LAUGHTER ON THE STAIRS

W. McLaren

BN

LAUGHTER ON THE STAIRS

Beverley Nichols

With a Foreword by Roy C. Dicks

TIMBER PRESS
Portland, Oregon

Dust jacket photograph of Beverley Nichols is the property of
Bryan Connon, reproduced with permission.

Drawings by William McLaren

First published in 1953 by Jonathan Cape

TIMBER PRESS, INC.
The Haseltine Building
133 S.W. Second Avenue, Suite 450
Portland, Oregon 97204, U.S.A.

Printed in Hong Kong

Library of Congress Cataloging-in-Publication Data

Nichols, Beverley, 1899–
    Laughter on the stairs / Beverley Nichols ; with a foreword by
Roy C. Dicks.
    p. cm.
    Originally published: London : J. Cape, 1953.
    Includes index.
    ISBN 0-88192-460-1
    I. Title.
PR6027.I22L3   1998
824'.912—dc21   98-7155
                                            CIP

CONTENTS

FOREWORD

OBSESSIONS are guilty pleasures to which we all succumb from time to time. My preoccupation with the writings of Beverley Nichols has been total and all-encompassing. With my background in gardening, writing, and theater, I was an easy mark.

A few years ago, Dr. J. C. Raulston, the late director of the North Carolina State University Arboretum, suggested I read Nichols's best-known gardening book, *Down the Garden Path*. (He also lent me Bryan Connon's biography *Beverley Nichols: A Life*, which is a must for the true enthusiast.) I was immediately taken with the humor and humanity of the writing—and the author's mischievous personality. My interest took quick root and soon I was on my way to collecting nearly all of Nichols's sixty books, including the twelve gardening titles, a task made more difficult by the fact that nearly all his books have been out of print for decades. I have even traveled to Britain to visit the four homes that provided the settings for his gardening books.

Though I do not expect every new reader to go to such extremes, I predict that most will not be able to stop reading Beverley Nichols after just one book. Few people who garden or have a love of nature will be able to resist the poetry, charm, and unabashed emotion with which Nichols invests his observations. First-time readers consistently report reactions that run something like "I have always secretly felt that way about gardening but thought I was the only one crazy enough to think such things!"

Originally, Nichols did not have any leanings toward gardening. He was already the author of nine books and numerous newspaper and magazine articles when he decided to "get away from it all" in 1928 by purchasing a small Tudor cottage in Glatton, about sixty miles north of London. The grounds were in such a dismal state that he decided to renovate the gardens. A complete novice learning by trial and error, he took three years to complete the project. He chronicled his failures, successes, and increasing enchantment with all plants and flowers in *Down the Garden Path* (1932). Due to the phenomenal public reaction, the book was quickly followed by two more titles about his cottage and garden, *A Thatched Roof* (1933) and *A Village in a Valley* (1934). As he moved to new locations during his life, he wrote of the gardens he developed at each site, publishing *Green Grows the City* (of his grounds at Hampstead), the Garden Open trilogy (Richmond), and my favorites, the Merry Hall trilogy.

Merry Hall was the name of a Georgian manor house twenty miles south of London near Ashtead, which Nichols purchased in 1945 after living in London for nine years. He wanted to have a bigger garden (Merry Hall was situated on four acres) and he wanted to have a grander home in which to entertain. He spent a large amount of money and time transforming the estate and the grounds into his personal haven. In 1951 he published *Merry Hall*, the first in the trilogy about his efforts there. *Laughter on the Stairs* and *Sunlight on the Lawn* were to follow in 1953 and 1956. For many, these are Nichols at his very best, mixing the archetypal sentiments of a gardener with flights of literary fancy and ripe British humor.

Some of the events and characters in these books were invented for dramatic effect, but the basic narrative is true and can be readily appreciated by anyone who gardens. *Laughter on the Stairs* has more to do with the house and the grounds and has fewer plant references than *Merry Hall*, but it nonetheless is full of quotable lines and clever phrases for the gardener. Seek out, for example, the "four L's of gardening" and the reason geraniums are a litmus test for one's moral rectitude. The hilarious final chapters concerning the competitiveness of a local flower show are sure to be vividly memorable.

I have lectured on Nichols for many groups and on many occasions, and it has been frustrating to be unable to direct audience members to copies of his works for purchase. I am pleased, therefore, that my obsession, in the form of research and indexing, has helped Timber Press to make these reprints possible. They should spark a renaissance of interest in all of Nichols's garden writings and help create a new generation of obsessives to keep me company.

Roy C. Dicks
Raleigh, North Carolina

LAUGHTER ON THE STAIRS

Facsimile of the Original Edition of 1953

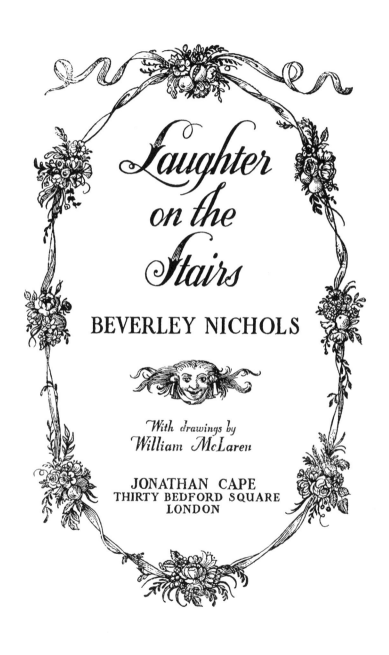

Laughter on the Stairs

BEVERLEY NICHOLS

With drawings by
William McLaren

JONATHAN CAPE
THIRTY BEDFORD SQUARE
LONDON

To
DOROTHY
The Lady of
WYCH
CROSS

CONTENTS

CHAPTER ONE

SPERO MELIORA

SPERO MELIORA proclaimed the stained-glass window on the stairs, in Gothic lettering against a background of raspberry pink, and I still had enough fourth-form Latin to remember that these words meant 'I hope for better things'. As indeed I did, each time that I passed it. It would have been beyond the bounds of reason to hope for worse.

Of all the horrors that the late Mr. Stebbing had perpetrated at Merry Hall, the stained-glass window was unquestionably the most alarming. It beat the plaster dwarfs that he had caused to lurk in the shrubbery; it beat the arrogant square window that he had erected, jutting out from the gracious Georgian façade; it beat the contraptions of shiny mauve tiles which he had stuffed into the wide old fireplaces. It even beat the enormous mound of earth which he had piled in the centre of the lawn, so that he might cover it with a rash of small brown rocks, composed of pebbles stuck together with cement.

I never met the late Mr. Stebbing; he died some five years before I bought the house; all that I knew about him was that he had a beard, that his favourite tree was a monkey puzzle, that he encouraged his dogs to chase cats, and that he played Liszt on an old pianola for half an hour every morning after breakfast, not because he liked music but because the action of pedalling was stimulating to his intestines. None of this information was calculated to endear him to me, even if his regrettable taste had not put me to an inordinate amount of expense in undoing everything that he had done. But it was impossible to escape from him; he haunted the house like a ghost. His name was constantly on the lips of Oldfield, my old gardener. He was for ever being held up as an example to me by Miss Emily Kaye, my most constant neighbour. And every time that I went upstairs, or came down again, or walked through the hall – stepping over the plaster and the rubble with which these early days were cluttered – he stared at me with an accusing glass eye, through a medley of blue, purple, pillar-box red, pink and slate. These, I suspect, were the colours of Mr. Stebbing's soul – particularly the slate. And it was his soul that the stained-glass window enshrined. It must go.

But when?

This is a simple story, which is lucky for both of us; I have never had much talent for devising complicated plots. All we will attempt to do is to carry the story of Merry Hall[1] from the garden to the house. It is as though we had been talking on the lawn and one of us had said: 'It's getting chilly; let's go indoors.' So in we go, and the talk continues. But this time it is of furniture rather than of flowers . . . of the carpets that have been woven by men, rather than those that have been stitched by the green fingers of nature . . . of the mirrors

[1] *Merry Hall*, by BEVERLEY NICHOLS (Jonathan Cape, 1951).

that were silvered by craftsmen two hundred years ago, rather than the mirrors of the water-garden, that tonight will be silvered by the frost. Needless to say, flowers will 'come in', as they always do, pushing and jostling into the life of every man who is primarily a gardener. There will be the shadow of a white cyclamen on the dark mahogany of my one piece of Chippendale; there will be petals trodden into my one Bokhara carpet, to say nothing of pieces of tarred twine and patches of mud. In the frozen depths of the mirror there will be the play and interplay of blossom, near and far, of the first daffodils that I offer it in March, of the shifting greens and bronzes of the copper beech that it echoes so lovingly in June, of the flames of the fires that flicker on the old hearths, from which the pale mauve tiles have long since been removed. (Have you ever noticed that a mirror reflects sound as well as sight? Have you ever stood before it, late at night, and stared into it, and listened to it? And heard all its sighs and its whispers, and all the secret refrains that are played in its far distances?)

'No,' you may say, with some sharpness, 'I have done no such thing.' Very well. If you are that sort of person, we both know where we are. I can continue to look into my mirrors, and you can continue to look into yours; we can both be delighted with the pictures we see therein; and we can take consolation in the thought that it takes all sorts to make a world.

§ I I

But when?

That was the question we were asking. When could we get rid of the stained-glass window?

Which reminds me that I have not yet described it.

It was about five feet tall and three feet wide, and since it was half way up the staircase in the hall, immediately opposite the front door, it threw ghastly shadows on to all who entered the house, giving them the appearance of messengers of doom. Its main colours were blue, mauve, pillar-box red, pink and slate. The central figure was an elderly gentleman in red, perched on a slate cloud, and looking exceedingly resentful about the whole business. To him, through a mélange of mauve lozenges, was ascending a well-proportioned young lady· with a mermaid's tail. At the base of the design were a number of mysterious symbols. There was something that might have been a spaniel; there were three ducks, one mauve, one pink, and one slate; there were several bars of music; and there were numerous signs that might have been Masonic symbols. Above the old gentleman's head, as we have already mentioned, was the inscription

SPERO MELIORA

Whether it was the old gentleman who hoped for better things than the mermaid, or the mermaid who hoped for better things than the old gentleman, I could never make up my mind. Perhaps it was Mr. Stebbing who was doing the hoping, and perhaps he was hoping for better things than either of them.

'But you must have been out of your mind,' you may tell me, 'not to have got rid of it at once.' Yes, I suppose I was, in a way. However, apart from its unique ugliness – which made it a sort of museum piece, so that one wondered whether it ought not to be preserved for posterity – there was another reason for my hesitation. There were, indeed, three reasons.

The first reason was Gaskin, my friend, familiar and factotum, who will be discovered in these pages in a number of agreeable roles, making omelettes, mowing lawns, giving pills to the cats, and telling outrageous lies on the telephone. 'Well, madam, I *think* Mr. Nichols has just gone out. If you'll just hold the line for a moment' . . . (Aside, to me: 'It's that mad woman at Woking, the one who wants you to go and stay in a caravan') ... 'I'm so sorry, madam, you've missed him, his car's just gone down the lane. No madam, I really couldn't say.'

When I told Gaskin that the stained-glass window must go, his reaction was immediate, and strongly hostile.

'What, *now*?' he exclaimed. 'Just when all the painting and papering's finished and the carpets are laid?'

'We could hammer it out ourselves, and push it into the garden so that it wouldn't make any mess.'

'Not make any mess?' Gaskin gave a distinct snort. 'And what about all the making good?'

Making good! It is a phrase which sends cold shudders down my back. One orders something to be done, like pulling down a picture rail, or ripping off a dado – something that surely could not be simpler – and then, when the picture rail is removed, half the wall comes down with it, and when the dado is removed it unlooses an avalanche of plaster and discloses a sinister hole that leads straight to the cellar. Whereupon, for several days, quantities of large young men in white jackets barricade themselves in the room, smoking Woodbines and drinking fantastic quantities of tea ... making good. And bang goes another fifty pounds.

'What Mr. Young will say, when you tell him, I simply do NOT know,' proclaimed Gaskin.

Mr. Young was another of the reasons why I hesitated. Mr. Young is the local builder and decorator who has lived for many years in the little house at the end of the lane; and though he does not pretend to be a man of culture, he has the heart of an artist. 'This is the sort of job a man dreams about,' he has sometimes said to me, when we have been planning something specially delectable. When we were putting the balustrading round the water-garden he got so excited that he twice stepped into it backwards.

On hearing about the stained-glass window, Mr. Young's face fell. 'It's the estimates,' he said. 'We've spent almost all our allowance. I don't know as how I could convince the Borough Surveyor that it was in the national interest.'

'Supposing I asked him to dine?'

Mr. Young did not think this was a very good idea.

'Supposing we threw a brick at the window and said it was war damage?'

Mr. Young did not think this was a very good idea, either.

'But it *is* in the national interest, Mr. Young.' I explained to him that sometimes, as an author, I tried to make people laugh. Not only in this country, but in America. And that sometimes, after a back-breaking effort on my part, they did at least emit a sort of gloomy cackle, for which they paid in dollars. If dollars were not in the national interest, what was . . . or rather, what were? How could one be funny with a thing like that about the house?

Mr. Young, with his artist's soul, was in complete agreement. But he still continued to shake his head. The Borough Surveyor, it seemed, was a tough nut to crack. The Borough Surveyor held very strong views about the National Interest. He was crazy about the National Interest. However, Mr. Young would try.

In the meantime, the glass eye continued to stare down at me, and the glass mermaid remained frozen against the dawns and the dusks. And I went on hoping for meliora.

§ III

But the third reason – in the shape of Miss Emily – was perhaps the most important of all.

Some of my readers will already have met my neighbour, the Honorable Emily Kaye. She is one of those thorns in the flesh from which one would part with reluctance; even when she is at her most maddening she never fails to stimulate. She is in her late thirties, aggressively healthy, rather tall, with prematurely greying hair, and fine but chilly eyes. She has a nice little income and a complete absence of taste – a combination which, one would have thought, would have ensured her a suitable husband. However, she has preferred to remain single, for a reason which she scarcely troubles to conceal. She cherishes a hopeless passion for the late Mr. Stebbing.

What an intelligent, well-bred woman like Miss Emily could have seen in a bearded monster like Mr. Stebbing, who was old enough to be her father, is a subject on which it would not be profitable to speculate. Perhaps it was because they had the same taste in decoration. To her, everything that Mr. Stebbing had done to the old house was perfection, and therefore everything that I had done was vandalism. When I removed the porcupine mound on the lawn, at enormous expense, she sulked for a week. When I tore down the cast-iron railings which he had erected on top of the little crescent wall outside the front door, she nearly wept. The climax came when I stripped off the wallpapers in the hall.

Wallpapers, not wallpaper; the plural is deliberate; there were no less than five wallpapers in the hall, which Mr. Stebbing had piled, one on top of another, throughout the years. At the bottom there was a pink chintzy one, and then a yellow one with blue butterflies, and then one which was apparently intended to give the illusion of lavatory tiles, and then a shiny green one with windmills on it, and finally an absolute beast of a thing which looked like a sort of fruit salad in the darkest shades of orange and maroon. This was the wallpaper that greeted me when I first stepped into Merry Hall; I tore it off with my own hands, bringing down a lot of plaster at the same time, and revealing the four minor horrors underneath.

Miss Emily caught me in the act, for the front door was open, and she had walked in, unasked, to pay a call, without troubling to ring the bell. This was not a habit which I felt inclined to encourage.

'Oh dear!' she cried in dismay. 'You're not changing *this*?'

'Yes – all of it.' And then, before she could reply ... 'I can't understand why Gaskin didn't come to let you in when you rang. I hope you weren't kept waiting long?'

She had the grace to be slightly confused. 'How silly of me! I entirely forgot that I should have rung. In the old days the front door was always kept on the latch ... one just wandered in. *Please* forgive me.'

'Not at all.' Whereupon I tore off another strip. It split in two, revealing a large square of the lavatory tiles.

Miss Emily covered her eyes with her hands. 'I seem to have come at *quite* the wrong moment. Each of those papers has its memory for me.'

'What I can't imagine,' I said, 'is why they were all stuck on top of one another.'

'If you had known Mr. Stebbing, you would have understood. *He* couldn't bear to destroy beautiful things. I remember so well that when the paper men were hanging the butterfly pattern, they wanted to strip off the chintz first. He was adamant. Quite adamant. He said that it had given him so many happy hours that it would be like tearing away part of himself.'

To such nonsense there was no reply. I tore off another strip.

'And what are we going to put up instead?' asked Miss Emily, when the dust had subsided.

'Plain white, I think.'

She shuddered, very slightly, but just enough to show me how she felt. Then she forced a brave smile to her lips. 'The dear old house will be quite modern by the time you have finished.'

'I don't think so. I'm only trying to restore it to what it was.'

'Really? With all these new ideas?'

'They're hardly new.'

'All this whiteness and brightness?'

'That's just pure eighteenth century.'

'Surely not.' She shook her head. By now we were both beginning to tremble with rage, though our smiles remained fixed to our faces, like rival hyenas. This, I should add, is our normal condition during most of our dialogues, which we both greatly enjoy.

'If you had ever read any books on eighteenth-century interiors . . .' I began.

'I have. Dozens.'

'Really! Which ones?'

'That is hardly to the point, is it?' I should have thought it was very much to the point, and was about to say so, but Miss Emily abruptly changed the subject. Stepping backwards, and turning her head, she gazed up at the stained glass window. 'Well, at least I can be thankful for one thing. We still have *this*.'

I did not dare to tell her how I felt about it, so I merely nodded.

'You do agree, don't you, that it does something to the house that nothing else could do?'

'I certainly do.'

'I'm so relieved.' Poor dear, she really was. It was a most difficult situation. Maddening as some women can be, one does not want to hurt them. I could not trust myself to make any comments on the window, as a work of art, so I asked her if there was any story connected with it.

'But hasn't anybody ever told you? *She* . . .' pointing to the mermaid . . . 'is the first Mrs. Stebbing.'

'But why a mermaid?'

'The first Mrs. Stebbing' – and there was a chill in Miss Emily's voice which suggested that she held a dim opinion of that lady – 'was on the stage. Not a very great success, I believe. She was dressed as a mermaid when Mr. Stebbing first saw her in the theatre.'

23

'I see. And is this a scene from the play?'

'From the play?' Miss Emily looked quite shocked. 'Certainly not. It is a sacred subject. She – the first Mrs. Stebbing – is ascending into Abraham's . . . ahem . . . bosom.'

So *that* was what it was, the small mauve triangle under the old gentleman's beard. It was Abraham's ahembosom. Who would have thought it? I had often pondered, in an absentminded sort of way, over this celebrated refuge, and had wondered what it would be like, if and when one reached it. I had looked forward to my own chances with somewhat mixed emotions, for I felt that Abraham's ahembosom must by now be somewhat overcrowded – in the same way that the knees of the gods must be somewhat threadbare.

'I see.' I longed to ask if Abraham himself was a portrait of the late Mr. Stebbing, but it might have been tactless. So I asked about the ducks instead.

'Oh – the ducks! Yes . . . aren't they darlings? They were Mr. Stebbing's especial favourites. Shadrek, Meshek and Abednego, they were called. They lived on the pond that is outside the music-room; at least, that *used* to be outside the music-room, before you filled it in. Whenever music was being played they used to join in, with the quaintest noises!'

The ghostly picture of the late Mr. Stebbing was becoming clearer and clearer as she spoke, and less and less alluring. Liszt, played on the pianola after breakfast, for the benefit of the intestines, was bad enough; the addition of the ducks made it quite horrifying.

'I wonder,' I asked, 'what the second Mrs. Stebbing thought of the window.'

Miss Emily drew in her breath, as she always did when the name of the second Mrs. Stebbing was mentioned.

'The second Mrs. Stebbing had no taste. None whatever.'

'Didn't she like it?'

'It wasn't a question of *liking*. She never argued with Mr. Stebbing about what she should like or dislike, not from an

24

artistic point of view. At least she knew better than *that!*'
I began to feel an affection for the second Mrs. Stebbing.
'She was an invalid,' continued Miss Emily, with mounting
resentment. 'Totally unsuited to a man of Mr. Stebbing's
virility. And she was very short-sighted. I shall never forget
the day she tripped on the stairs, and broke her ankle, and
complained because she had an idea that the window shut out
the light! It upset Mr. Stebbing terribly.'
'It must have upset Mrs. Stebbing too, to some extent.'
Miss Emily answered this retort with a disdainful sniff.
'She also seemed to feel some sort of resentment against the
motto.'
'Spero meliora?'
'Yes. It came from Mr. Stebbing's family crest. Such a
charming sentiment, I always think, hoping for better things.
But Mrs. Stebbing seemed to think that it was in some way a
reflection upon herself. When people came to call, she used to
make quite sarcastic comments on it. And *that* upset Mr.
Stebbing, for naturally it had a very special meaning for him.'
I should have liked to suggest that perhaps it had a very
special meaning for the mermaid too, but it was not the sort of
remark that Miss Emily would have appreciated.
'Well,' she said, 'I mustn't stay here, interrupting you with
your work. But before I go, I wonder . . . might I have just a
tiny piece of the wallpaper? For a souvenir?'
'Of course. But I'm afraid it's all stuck together.'
'I can steam it apart quite easily. Then I can mount the
five separate pieces in my album. Thank you so much.' She
stroked it affectionately. Then she turned and waved to the
window. 'Goodbye. I *am* so glad that you are not taking it
down. Do you know, I believe that if you had done, some
terrible thing would have happened.'
'Such as?'
She looked me straight in the eye. 'I believe that you would
have been haunted.'

§ I V

When she had gone, the house suddenly seemed very hushed and still.

Well, I thought, I *am* being haunted. Haunted by Mr. Stebbing. And Miss Emily is his creature, whom he is controlling from Abraham's ahembosom. And the proof of his power lies in the fact that because of her my hands are tied. I dare not flout her – not yet.

I walked slowly up the first three steps of the old staircase, whose delicate balustrade had only just been stripped of the coats of coarse brown paint with which the late Mr. Stebbing had encrusted it. I gazed up at the window. The rays of the dying sun glinted through the eye of Abraham – that is to say, through the eye of the late Mr. Stebbing – and fixed me with an accusing glare. It also shone through the eyes of the ducks, and the eyes of the spaniel, and if the mermaid had been able to turn her head, it would certainly have also shone through hers. As it was, it shone through her behind, which was pale pink and extremely hostile.

'Well,' I said to Abraham, alias Mr. Stebbing, 'the fight is on. The gloves are off. Nichols versus Stebbing. That's how it's going to be.'

Mr. Stebbing continued to glare. Of course, I ought to have taken a brick at that very moment and hurled it through his shining amber beard. But that wouldn't have seemed very sporting. After all, the late Mr. Stebbing was dead. He could not answer back. He was impotent, immobile. Crystallized up there, on the staircase, in all his ghastly majesty. But dead? No. There was still a power about him. He could still darken my dawns and poison my dusks. It would need a stronger hand than mine . . . in all the curious circumstances of these first days . . . to destroy him.

That hand, though I did not know it, was about to strike.

CHAPTER TWO

THIEVES IN THE NIGHT

SINCE the burglary was one of the few really unpleasant
things that ever happened at Merry Hall, and since it led,
more or less directly, to a great many changes in the house
and in our habits of life, we had better get it over as soon as
possible.

It happened at about nine o'clock on a hot Saturday night in
late September, some few weeks after we had moved in. For
once in a way the house was entirely deserted; Oldfield had
gone his rounds, Gaskin was in the 'local', my old friend Cyril –
an ex-naval type who would have been extremely useful –
had gone to the movies. I was some miles away, playing
canasta with Miss Emily and her friend Rose Fenton at Rose's
ultra-Tudor cottage, which was called The Weathercocke.
Yes, I do mean *the* Rose Fenton – the one whose photograph
you have so often seen in the papers, judging flower shows,
lecturing on flower-arrangement, or standing, with a smirk of
satisfaction, by the side of one of her floral creations, which
are invariably appalling. I dote on Rose as a person; she is
round and soft and cosy; she makes a perfect dry Martini –

three-quarters of gin one-quarter of French vermouth, a squeeze of lemon peel and masses of ice – and she is generous to a fault. But when she arranges flowers she massacres them. An example of her handiwork had been staring at me throughout the evening; it was a sort of pyramid of pom-pom dahlias standing on an oldy-worldy copper plate; it was almost solid and the heads of the lower flowers were completely chopped off. In the top of it she had stuck a small piece of asparagus fern, like a feather. This arrangement had been created for my especial benefit, and Rose had constantly glanced from it to me, and from me to it, waiting for compliments. She did not get any.

Our fourth was one of our most charming neighbours, whom we all know as Marius – a nickname that he earned at Oxford, where he was one of the most brilliant scholars of his generation. Since he is a real person, of a diffident nature, and since his profession – not quite Foreign Office, not quite Secret Service, but a little of both – is one which discourages publicity I will not paint too detailed a picture of him. It is enough to imagine a man of thirty-five, tall, dark, and apparently languid. I say 'apparently' because though Marius walks slowly, and stoops and sometimes stutters, there is nothing at all languid about his mind. As some gentlemen on the wrong side of the Iron Curtain have discovered to their cost.

The game was waxing fast and furious; an enormous pack, which had been 'frozen' and 'refrozen', had piled up on the table; everybody was in that state of acute agony and nervous tension which makes canasta the most exquisite torture ever devised for man's delight. Then the telephone rang.

Rose paused, holding back the card which she had been about to throw. Her hand was trembling violently. 'It's too bad!' she cried. 'To ring up at a time like this! People have no consideration.'

'None,' agreed Miss Emily in a shaking voice. 'But please throw, darling. This suspense is killing me.'

The telephone rang again. 'I *can't* go,' wailed Rose. 'I shall forget everything that has been thrown.' She turned to me. 'Would you be an angel?'

I went out into the little hall and lifted the receiver. It was Gaskin, in a state of great agitation. The house had been broken into, and heaven knows what wasn't missing, and – no, nobody was hurt, and – yes, 'One' and 'Four' were quite all right, in fact they had slept through it all, but would I please come home at once?

I rang off. This was obviously an occasion for *sang-froid*. (*Sang-froid*, I always find, is much easier to assume than one imagines. On the few occasions in life when it has been needed I have produced it in such quantities that I have been quite astonished. Always provided, of course, that there is somebody there to watch.)

So it was now. I went back into the room. 'I'm afraid that I shall have to break up the party.'

Violent protests from Rose and Miss Emily. It was unthinkable – monstrous – at a moment like this.

'He's not serious,' quavered Miss Emily. 'Rose darling, play your card.'

I hesitated a moment, and then sat down.

Rose played her card. It was the one card that gave me the pack . . . and the game. Never was so much *sang-froid* displayed in the history of mankind. I took up the pack, and counted out no less than seven canastas, to the accompaniment of a torrent of recrimination from the two ladies.

Then I got up again. 'And now I really must go. My house has been burgled. No, I don't think anybody has been *seriously* hurt. How much? I couldn't say. Not much more than a thousand pounds worth, I hope. No . . . please don't bother. I can find my own way.'

Exit, feeling so much like Sydney Carton that I was quite surprised not to see a tumbril waiting at the door.

§ 11

At Merry Hall, confusion. All the lights were on, and the music-room was a shambles. At the end of this room there was a strong cupboard with a barred window; the burglars had hacked their way through the door and taken the safe which had stood there. You could see the ridges in the felt where they had dragged it across the floor. There had been a great deal in that safe that was precious to me, not only financially but sentimentally.

'Lay not up for yourself treasures on earth,' I reflected – somewhat belatedly – as I stood there, blinking at the emptiness. 'Or if you do, see that your insurance policies are up-to-date.' Mine, needless to say, were not.

Meanwhile Gaskin was running here, there and everywhere, returning every other minute with news of some fresh disaster. First it was the typewriter that had gone. Then a radio set. Then some gold cuff-links. Then three brand new suits which, ironically enough, had arrived from the tailors that very morning and had never even been worn. Finally the gloomy catalogue was complete, and he came in and sat down with me and Cyril, awaiting the arrival of the police.

Now was obviously the occasion for a really shattering display of *sang-froid*. So I lit a cigarette, endeavoured to achieve a yawn . . . which ended in a sort of gulp . . . and said, 'We mustn't touch anything till the police come.'

'Oh no,' agreed Gaskin. 'We mustn't touch anything.'

Cyril too was very emphatic that we mustn't touch anything. We had evidently been reading the same detective stories.

So we sat there, staring about us, not touching anything. It got on my nerves.

'We can't sit here like dummies, not touching things,' I said. 'It's so negative.'

'I could touch a drink,' suggested Cyril.

30

'You can't,' retorted Gaskin. 'They've taken the whole lot.'

'Oh Lord!' snorted Cyril. 'That's the worst news yet.'

In view of the contents of my safe, this seemed to me an exaggeration, but I was too busy with my *sang-froid* to say so. Instead, I said:

'I wonder who could possibly have done it?'

As soon as this unfortunate question was out of my mouth, I regretted it. It seemed to ring round the room with an awful echo, involving us all in a common guilt. Never, never, if you have a burglary, say 'Whodunnit?' Not in so many words. Nobody can look his neighbour in the face, after the question has been put. That simple word 'Whodunnit?' immediately transforms your burglary into an Agatha Christie detective story, of which the main point is invariably that the one person who could not have dunnit is the one person who did.

Thus, though Gaskin could no more have dunnit than the President of the United States, he immediately gave a startling impersonation of guilt, and looked at me with a curiously furtive expression. Cyril was rather less likely to have dunnit than Mr. Winston Churchill, but his normally open countenance assumed a distinctly hangdog air. Even 'One' and 'Four', who had hitherto been prowling about with the greatest enjoyment, sniffing the broken woodwork, dabbing at the fallen plaster, suddenly drooped their tails and slunk away, looking for all the world as though *they* had dunnit.

So we sat there, and went on sitting, waiting for the police, feeling more and more like confederates in the crime.

Suddenly a question occurred to me – a question so obvious that it should have been asked at the very beginning.

'But how did they get in?'

Gaskin hesitated for a moment, as though he were reluctant to tell me. Then he said: 'Through the stained-glass window.'

My heart gave a jump. For a moment I forgot all about the messes and the losses and the confusions. I ran out into the hall, and up the staircase.

§ III

The burglars had entered through the mermaid's behind.

The reader may remember that this object was large, pink, and hexagonal, ideally constructed for such purposes. Having removed the behind – which, with a curious solicitude, they had propped up on the ledge, where it stared at me with a most sinister expression – they had proceeded to remove the head of the spaniel, the breasts of two of the ducks, and part of the bar of music. These objects had fallen on to the carpet, where I let them remain.

But there was one piece of the glass which had rolled down the stairs, on to the bottom step, where it caught the full force of the naked light which still dangled from the ceiling. A small, oval piece of glass, grey-blue, the size of a starling's egg. It glared and glittered at me, as though it were alive, and as I watched it, it seemed to wink.

It was the eye of Abraham, the eye of the late Mr. Stebbing, and it was at my mercy.

I stepped forward to pick it up. Then I paused. One must not touch things. But surely this was a rather exceptional case? The late Mr. Stebbing's eye could not have any special significance for the police. It could not compare, in importance, with the first Mrs. Stebbing's behind. *That* was the object through which the evil-doers had made their entrance . . . the eye was merely a detail, which could be of little interest to them.

But it was of the greatest possible interest to me. With this in my possession, I felt that I had the late Mr. Stebbing where I wanted him. He could no longer hypnotize me and dominate me, as he had obviously hypnotized and dominated the first and second Mrs. Stebbings.

I picked up the eye, and put it in my waistcoat pocket. I should not have been surprised if it had suddenly begun to twitch, or grow hot, or start making some horrible sort of hiss.

At the moment it showed no sign of doing such things; perhaps it was biding its time. Meanwhile, my thoughts were diverted by the arrival of the police.

The police could not have been more charming. There were three of them, a large grey one, a small beige one, and a gigantic, very red, very young one. (I seem, inadvertently, to have been describing a trio of gladioli, but let it pass.) They stepped about the music-room like dancers on a stage, they waved tape measures, they flashed lights, they peered into corners, they tapped window-panes with gloved fingers. I watched them, enthralled. So did Cyril and Gaskin. And, of course, 'One' and 'Four'. It was long past the cats' bedtime; they should have been curled up on the kitchen chair, with 'One's' arm round 'Four's' neck, and a general mingling of tails and whiskers. Instead, they sat straight up in the fireplace, very bright-eyed, missing nothing.

Then we were finger-printed, by the small beige policeman. He did it with such finesse that one felt that it was quite a privilege to have one's thumb stuck into a lot of ink, in one's own house, at two o'clock in the morning.

And then out came the notebooks and we were cross-examined. Where had we been? What had we been doing? How long had we stayed? When had we left? It was all conducted with the greatest courtesy; we all had excellent alibis, and fortunately we had been passing the most respectable evenings. Even so, by the time we had given all our answers, we sounded like a collection of debauchees.

The large red policeman was the last to go. As we said good night I pointed to the litter of glass on the staircase.

'By the way, inspector, can we clear this glass away now?'

'That'll be quite all right, sir.' He looked up at the shattered window. 'You'll be putting it back again, I expect?'

'I'm not quite sure. Perhaps in some other place.'

''Twould be a pity to waste a beautiful piece of glass like

that.' He stepped forward and stared at the pink hexagon which had been detached from the first Mrs. Stebbing.

'Funny,' he said. 'That bit seems sort of familiar. I wonder what it is.'

'Just a part of . . . of the design.'

'Very funny. I could swear I'd seen it before somewhere.'

He took his leave. As the front door closed after him, the eye in my waistcoat pocket gave a distinct twitch.

§ I V

I was too tired to sleep, so I wandered out into the garden. The moon was high, and the old house, dreaming there among the lilies and the roses, looked as though its tranquillity had been unbroken through the centuries. I had a sense of indignation on its behalf, quite apart from my own loss. It was such a gracious old place, so gentle, so harmless, so welcoming – it seemed monstrous that a gang of criminals should steal towards it at night, and shatter its dream, and crash through its feeble defences. As the years go by, an old house gathers an aura of pride; through many winters of discontent it has braved the windy nights and the rainy morrows; through many summers, long forgotten, it has shielded its owners from the heat of the day; and the old brick walls are lit with a glow of satisfaction. Even the chimneys, I fancy, have a jaunty tilt to them . . . like the bonnets of old ladies who have had hard lives, but have conquered them – old ladies who still walk down the street with an expression that seems to say, 'Let 'em all come!'

The old house, I was sure, must be feeling hurt and wounded. Well, we would have to make up for it, somehow or other, in the days to come; we would have to do something which it would like very much indeed, such as putting a beautiful fanlight over its front door. However, I have so often been told that it is sloppy and sentimental to invest inanimate objects with human sentiments, that I had better change the subject, preferably to something 'hard' and 'brittle' and 'sophisticated'.

Which might well be the cue for the entry of the four gold cigarette cases.

There had been four gold cigarette cases in that safe, three of them from the elegant house of Monsieur Cartier, and as I prowled about on the moonlit lawns I began to feel more and more resentful about their loss. You may tell me that four gold cigarette cases is an inordinate number for a struggling author, but they had been bought as an investment, in a desperate endeavour to find something that would not 'go down'. I do not recall that I have ever made any investment in anything whatsoever that has not instantly 'gone down', with the possible exception of gin, and that goes down, in another sense, all too swiftly. Shares are fatal, no matter how eminent the advice on which I have acted. Once, for example, I bought some shares in a whaling company; within the hour all the whales had obviously heard of the transaction, for they rushed helter-skelter to the ends of the earth, where they remained sulking at the bottom of the sea until I had sold my interests. On both of the occasions when I bought gold mining shares the managing directors were arrested on the following day, in a welter of fraud, corruption and bankruptcy. My purchase of oil shares usually involves either a national insurrection, an explosion at the refinery, the suicide of the chief engineer, or all three.

As for 'gilt-edged', the only shares I ever owned bearing this comic description were purchased from a deplorable man called Mr. Dalton, who was one of the first Socialist Chancellors of the Exchequer. They shot from £100 to £60 – which, for me, was almost equivalent to a profit. But it was hardly 'gilt-edged'.

Hence the gold cigarette cases. I bought them at Cartier's

in the middle of an air-raid. It was a queer sensation, standing in that little jewel-box in Bond Street, with the soft carpet underneath one's feet, and all the bangs and smoke outside. The cases were quite beautiful, and utterly unreal, in the circumstances. There was a heavy ribbed one, with a big sapphire for a clip. And a very tiny one, with a design like frost flowers on a window-pane. And one which was very plain and chaste, with a slim border of platinum. The young man said – apparently with no *arrière pensée* – that it would be 'suitable for country use'.

Yes, I thought, very suitable. One could flash it out of one's tweeds before aiming at otters, or whatever most of Cartier's clients do in the country.

And there was one other, in some ways the prettiest of all. It was Viennese, of the late eighteenth century, with a design of fleur de lys. It was fashioned in a very pale shade of gold, and on the inside of the lid, in a spidery handwriting, were engraved the words *Toi pour moi, et moi pour toi.*

Those cigarette cases, apart from their intrinsic beauty, had given me a curious sense of security out of all proportion to their value in cash. I have never been able to look very far ahead, in material affairs, and somehow I had felt that as long as I had the cases, there was nothing to worry about. If Britain were to be invaded, which was probable, and if one were put in a concentration camp, which in view of one's record was certain, one could bury the cigarette cases in the rhubarb bed before setting off for the local Belsen, and they would give one a nice glow of satisfaction throughout the period of incarceration.

But now, one felt naked and defenceless. And though the immediate danger of invasion appeared to have retreated, one never knew when it might not come again. At any moment the silent skies might swarm with life, and darken with a thousand bat-like shapes floating down to the moonlit lawns. Which reminded me that a bat-like shape had just skimmed very low over my head. If one of them were to fix itself in my hair, not all the *sang-froid* in the world would prevent me from an unmanly display of hysteria. So I said good night to the garden and went to bed.

§ v

On the following morning, the first thing we did was to attack the stained-glass window in force.

'This is the sort of thing I've been longing to do all my life,' said Cyril, hoisting himself on to the ledge, and brandishing a hammer. 'Which bit shall we do first?'

'Let's finish off the mermaid.'

'The best bit's gone. But we can give her a nice one in the neck.'

Crash!

'Now I'm going to polish off these ruddy ducks.'

Crash, crash, crash!

The last to go was the motto, which hung precariously on two scrolls of lead. Cyril took the SPERO and I took the MELIORA and they both went skimming into the garden in a flurry of flying letters. When I went out to clear up the mess I saw that eight of the letters had grouped themselves on the grass in a sort of anagram . . .

SOAP MORE!

Perhaps it was Mr. Stebbing's last gesture of defiance.

Gaskin brought a sack and we shovelled the glass into it.

'Whatever will Miss Emily think?' asked Gaskin.

'We mustn't give her a chance of thinking anything. We must say that the burglars took the whole lot.'

'She'll never get over it.'

'Oh yes, she will. In a way it's a sort of compliment to her. She'll be able to say that it was such a masterpiece that the

37

burglars came specially for it. And that they only went off with the safe as a sort of afterthought.'

I carried the sack over to Oldfield, who was in the greenhouse, tying up his chrysanthemums.

'I want you to bury this somewhere,' I said to him.

He took the sack. 'This'll be t'window? Aye. I'll bury it good and deep.'

'Didn't you like it either?'

He shook his head. 'Proper place for stained-glass windows is t'chapel. I'll bury it good and deep.' He kicked the sack into a corner, sighed, straightened himself, and folded his arms. ''Tis a pity I wasn't around last night.'

'In some ways it's a good thing you weren't, Oldfield. The police say there must have been four of them. And they may have been armed.'

'Pshaw!' He wrinkled his old nose in a gesture of contempt. 'I'd 'ave given 'em something to think on if there'd been forty.'

There was evidently more in his indignation than met the eye. It was not long in revealing itself.

'They've done in two of t'best camellias.' His voice trembled with grief and rage. 'Aye! Drove right over 'em.'

This was bad news indeed. The planting of those camellias was one of the few signs of taste which the late Mr. Stebbing had ever shown. I can only assume that he had planted them by mistake, in the delusion that they were laurels. They were grouped in the shadow of some tall lilacs in the drive. Alas, Oldfield had not been exaggerating. The burglars had backed their car right over the two finest bushes, the pink and white striped ones that I loved so much. The stems were split in half, and they were beyond hope.

'Only yesterday morning,' quavered Oldfield, 'I gave 'em a top-dressing of leaf mould. And some flowers of sulphur, on account of t'lime. They can't abide lime. And now. . . .'

It was maddening, but I didn't want the old man to break

his heart about it. 'Never mind,' I said. 'I'll buy some more.'

'Aye!' he said, with more than a hint of scorn. 'You can buy some more. But you can't buy the years they've been a'growing. You can't buy time.'

I sighed. It was all too true.

'You can't buy time,' he repeated, fixing me with an accusing eye. ''Twas Thomas Edison as said that.' A pause, and then an unexpected chuckle. 'I reckon Mister Edison must have been a gardener.'

While we had been standing there I noticed out of the corner of my eye that a car had driven up to the front of the house. Out of it stepped two familiar figures, Miss Emily and Our Rose. I left Oldfield with his stricken camellias and went inside to greet the visitors.

When I opened the door of the music-room, both ladies were bending low over an urn of mixed flowers which, though I say it myself, was rather sensational. The flowers were held in place by a complicated contraption of wire with a base of fine sand and – well, certain other things which I cannot be induced to divulge in public. Our Rose had often hinted that she would like to be let into the secret, but I had always managed to avoid telling her. And there she was, spying. Shamelesser and shamelesser.

Slightly flushed, the ladies turned to offer their sympathies.

'We felt we *had* to come,' said Miss Emily.

'Such a hateful thing to happen,' added Our Rose.

'Gaskin has told us about the window. An absolute tragedy.'

'There was quite a lot else that they took,' I said.

'Yes, yes. Very upsetting, I know. But the *window* was unique.'

'Yes. Of course.'

'Obviously, that was what they came for. Gaskin tells me that not a single piece of glass was left.'

'Well . . .' I thought of the first Mrs. Stebbing's hexagonal behind, which the burglars had propped up on the ledge. I also thought of Mr. Stebbing's eye, which was still in my pocket, and wondered how Miss Emily would react if I suddenly took it out and waved it at her. I resisted the temptation.

'Not a thing.'

Miss Emily nodded. 'That proves it. It must have been a gang of art thieves. Probably Americans.' She shrugged her shoulders, and sat down heavily on the sofa. 'Really, with this government, one doesn't know where one is.'

'What else did they take?' asked Our Rose.

'There was the safe.'

'No? I never knew you had a safe.'

'I didn't know that *anybody* knew I had a safe. But obviously I was mistaken.'

'Was there much in it?'

'It was stuffed to the hilt with Cartier cigarette cases.'

Both ladies gasped. Then they realized that I was being 'amusing'.

'No . . . but really?'

'Just some money. And some bits and pieces.'

'It isn't the *money* value of the things that matters,' proclaimed Our Rose loftily.

No, I agreed. Though I had mental reservations about that.

'After all, *money* can be replaced.'

So it could, I said. More mental reservations.

'It's the *sentiment*. So many things – worthless things to other people – that must be irreplaceable.'

At which point the mental reservations became quite considerable. However, it might not be wise to mention them.

'No,' I agreed aloud. 'The actual value, of course, doesn't count. It's the sentiment.'

At which both ladies gravely nodded their heads. One had said the Right Thing.

But now a sharper note intruded, and I began to realize the true purpose of their visit.

'Nothing like this has ever happened in Meadowstream before,' said Our Rose.

'Never,' echoed Miss Emily.

'But surely there must have been *some* burglaries?' I ventured.

'None,' asserted Our Rose. 'Quite unheard of.'

'Quite,' agreed Miss Emily. 'Mr. Stebbing never even bothered to *close* the doors at Merry Hall, let alone lock them. Anybody could have walked in. Nobody ever did. He *trusted* people.'

'Perhaps he hadn't got anything worth stealing?'

Miss Emily, as I should have guessed, took this as a personal affront.

'Nothing worth *stealing*?' she echoed. And then, with a distinct snort, 'Merry Hall used to be a Treasure House.' No doubt it was coincidence that as she uttered these words her eyes fell on the hole in the blue felt, which was usually covered by the log basket. And having rested there for a moment, alighted on an ashtray which had been – I regret to admit – stolen from a wagon-lit on the Blue Train. It was badly cracked.

'A veritable Treasure House,' she repeated. 'For instance, there were Mrs. Stebbing's opals.'

'I thought that those were always kept at the bank?' interjected Our Rose, with less tact than usual.

'No dear.' Miss Emily shook her head sharply. 'Not at the bank. In the wall-safe.'

'But if he trusted people so much . . .' I began.

'And Mr. Stebbing's pewter,' interrupted Our Rose, making up for her previous tactlessness.

'Yes indeed. His pewter.'

'But do you think any burglar would have gone off with that?' I asked.

'Gone off with it?' Miss Emily arched her eyebrows. 'It was unique!'

'Tell him about what the South Kensington Museum said about it,' prompted Our Rose.

'I don't think he'd be interested in what the South Kensington Museum said about it.'

This was so poignantly true that I did not deny it.

'Well, all I can say,' observed Our Rose, with a happy sigh, 'is thank heavens for James and Jasmine!'

James and Jasmine, I should explain, are two gigantic Alsatians, of reputed ferocity, who guard Our Rose's Tudory Cottage. I say 'reputed' ferocity because on the only occasion that Our Rose brought them to my house they were met, in the hall, by 'One', who at that time was ten weeks old. It might be thought that a small and still somewhat tottery Siamese kitten, when suddenly confronted by two such mammoths, would have turned tail and fled. On the contrary. 'One', arching his back so that he stood at least seven inches from the floor, erecting his tail so that it looked like an outraged feather, and howling defiance in a squeak that could be heard at least three feet away, staggered towards them, squinting with rage. Whereupon the ferocious ones, after exchanging glances, beat an ignominious retreat, with their tails between their legs.

My opinion of 'One', which was already high, went higher. My affection for James and Jasmine, which had previously been qualified, was established on a firm basis. I like people whose barks are worse than their bites. James and Jasmine evidently belonged to this category. And I have always been impatient with this ridiculous war between cat and dog. I have a shrewd suspicion that the humans are largely responsible for it. At any rate, on this occasion, it was 'One' who was gently reprimanded, and given a token slap which transformed itself into a stroke, for being so discourteous to the canine visitors.

So I said yes, we must indeed thank heavens for James and Jasmine, and that it would be a sorry day for any burglar who should cross their path. After a few more hints that my burglary was quite unprecedented, that my coming to Meadowstream was directly responsible for a crime wave, that neither of the ladies would be able to sleep at nights and that both of them would be put to considerable expense by being obliged to fix new bolts and bars on doors and windows, they took their departure. As they walked down the steps towards their car, they both glanced nervously to the left and right, as though a band of brigands was crouched in the hedge, waiting to spring upon them. I could not help being reminded of the behaviour of the ladies of Cranford on a somewhat similar occasion, and how the immortal Miss Pole had offered a whole shilling to the bearers of the sedan chair if they would take the route that led from Darkness Lane to Headingley Causeway. Plus ça change. . . .

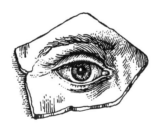

CHAPTER THREE

FENESTRALIA

IT was in more senses than one that the burglars opened a
new window into my life, and for that my thanks are
largely due to Marius.

So far, we have only met Marius as a rather dim figure at
the canasta table. On that occasion he did not speak, which
was a pity, for Marius is seldom a bore. His 'entertainment
value' lies in his erudition, and the lightness with which he
wears it. He sometimes puts me in mind of the young Aldous
Huxley. Aldous had a genius for evoking from the most
unlikely objects the spirit of their period, and for reuniting
them with the historical figures – often obscure – who had
been associated with them. In the dusky glass of a rococo
mirror he could see the shadow of ancient battles; he could

44

trace the beginning of a nation's decadence in the scroll of a picture frame, and find the outlines of a philosophy in the border of an Aubusson carpet. So it is with Marius. He constantly wanders through the rooms of my house and down the paths of my garden, and wherever he goes he leaves delicate scraps of knowledge in his wake. To follow him around is a sort of mental paper-chase. It was some days after the burglary before he came to offer his condolences. There was a rumour that he had been in Prague, rescuing bishops with one hand and bribing commissars with the other, but he seldom discusses his private affairs. He strolled into the drawing-room, where Cyril and I were scraping off the last traces of perhaps the most hideous wallpaper of the lot, a sort of willow-pattern in pale pink.

His opening gambit was typical. He bent over a bucket of paste which we had mixed as a sample for the paper-hangers, pushed his finger into it, and sniffed.

'Did you make this yourself?'

'Yes, Marius, we did.'

He beamed his approval. 'George Washington could not have made it better.'

I winked at Cyril; Marius was evidently in good form.

'What has George Washington to do with it?'

Marius seated himself upon a packing case. 'I know very little American history, and scarcely anything about George Washington, but I do know that he was an expert paper-hanger. Surely that is common knowledge?'

I wondered. As Marius was speaking, a cart rolled by in the lane outside, bearing six farm labourers on their way home. They all looked exceptionally vacant; all their mouths were wide open; and I very much doubt whether they knew anything whatever about George Washington and his paper-hanging proclivities. However, this was not the moment to remind Marius that what he regarded as 'common knowledge' was not always so common as he imagined.

'The President's great moment came,' continued Marius, 'when Martha Washington was expecting a visit from General Lafayette. She had ordered a new wallpaper for the occasion – and very bright and pretty it was, with paeonies and grapevines and parrots and crimson roses. (You doubtless know the pattern.) But the wallpaper, alas, did not arrive till Lafayette was already installed.'

'So what happened?'

'The two generals turned paper-hangers. Washington, in particular, busied himself with the manufacture of the paste. He was greatly concerned lest it should contain any lumps. He did not like lumps, in any shape or form. He even wrote a little brochure on the subject, with some quite heated injunctions on the absolute necessity of using glue on whitewashed walls.'

'Well,' said Cyril, 'we live and learn.'

'One would like to think so,' sighed Marius. 'But does one? What does one really know about wallpaper. Practically nothing. The barest outlines . . . foolish little scraps, like the story of the rats at Christ's.'

Cyril had been about to resume his attack on the willow-pattern, but he put his scraper down for the moment. 'Rats?' he echoed. 'Christ's?'

Marius gave him a glance of reproof. 'Sometimes I suspect that your ignorance is deliberately assumed.'

'I wasn't at Cambridge, Marius. Why should I have heard about the rats at Christ's?'

He shrugged his shoulders. 'I should have thought everybody had heard of them.'

'Tell us.'

'Very well. It was in the year 1518. The monarch of the moment – (in case you had forgotten!) – was Henry the Eighth.'

'Thank you. I got just as far as him at prep school.'

Marius bowed. 'To the Master of Christ's was delivered a

46

large bundle of a new invention, wallpaper. It bore a crude and lusty design on a dark blue ground – it was all a'flourish and afire, like Tudor England. One of the rolls, by some mistake, was left in a powder-closet. The powder-closet was walled up, and with it, the rats that had taken refuge there. The poor creatures ate the wallpaper – and I will not insult your intelligence by reminding you that there are certain acids in the stomach of the domestic rat which act as a preservative for the chemicals which were used in the dyes of the sixteenth century.'

'Marius, you are excelling yourself.'

He laughed. 'And we are both pulling each other's legs. But – seriously – I think it is exciting. Don't you? Tudor England. All its stench and splendour. The frightened little animals in the Master's Lodge. The scrapings, the nibblings, and then the silence for over four hundred years. And at last, the wall is broken down, and the light floods in, and a puzzled workman, with a cigarette in his mouth, sees a mound of bones that are almost dust, and among them, some fragments of faded paper. Paper that is stamped with the outline of a rose, the edge of a thistle, the tracing of a leaf. He scoops up the paper, and takes it downstairs to the Master . . . but I am boring you.'

'Far from it.'

'In that case, I might be persuaded to have a cocktail. And I might also be persuaded to deliver a short lecture on windows, which I am sure you will agree are very important.'

§ I I

Cyril and Marius went off to make the cocktail. I strolled over to one of the windows, sat on the ledge, and looked out.

'Yes,' I thought. 'Windows are very important.'

I wish you could have been with me at that moment, looking out through the window, to have seen the bareness and the desolation of it all; and I wish you could be with me now to see something – well, rather different. It was a wild October evening, with an angry glow behind the yellowing elms. Outside, there was an ugly wilderness of weeds and brambles; with here and there a tiny patch which we had begun to clear. But such was my faith that I saw it all as a garden; perhaps it might be far away, but I could still see it, a garden with smooth lawns, and trim hedges, and secret plots, and balustrades of silver stone. For these things I was prepared to fight, with whatever resources I could muster; if that garden did not come into being, I should have failed in life. And if you had been sitting there – with the wind rattling the decrepit window-frames and the first drops of rain spotting the glass – you would have noticed that the outside walls of the old house were empty and naked, scarred with a thousand rusting nails, to which Mr. Stebbing had tied the speckled ivies which we had been obliged to tear away. Yet I could see those walls made smooth and perfect again, and rioting with roses – roses whose leaves should tap on the panes, roses whose perfume would drift into the room, whose shadows would fall on my desk . . . as they fall at this moment, on my manuscript, in a delicate filigree that I fear may be resulting in a slight confusion of thought.

Yes, it seemed to me, windows were of the utmost importance. For they are the crystal link between our two lives, the life of the sun and the stars, and the life of the fire and the candle. They beckon to us and tempt us; they warn us and hold us back. It is infinitely regrettable that Shelley never wrote a poem about them; they might have given him a simile that would have shone, even more radiantly, than his immortal dome of many coloured glass.

These thoughts – luckily for the reader – were interrupted by the return of Marius and Cyril, bearing an outsize in dry martinis. After one sip, Marius blinked, and sat down heavily on the kitchen chair.

48

'My lecture on windows,' he proclaimed, 'would naturally begin with Jezebel.'

'Why Jezebel?'

'She was the first person to see their dramatic possibilities. When she painted her face and sat down in a window, she obviously had her eye on posterity. If she'd merely called out to Jehu across the courtyard, nobody would have remembered her. But she rouged her lips and darkened her eyes and went to the window, and called out through the lattice. There she is, framed for ever, with Jehu looking up at her, and the eunuchs gathering behind her. She was a very clever girl. You must read *Fenestralia*.'

'What is *Fenestralia*?'

'It is a very charming essay by a gentleman called Max Beerbohm, of whom you may conceivably have heard. It is all about windows, in art and in history, and the use that men have made of them. And women too. Until I read it I never realized why every amateur actress longs to play Juliet. It is because of the window. However incompetent she may be, she can't go wrong in *that*. All the same, I wish that I could have spoken to Max before he wrote it.' Marius frowned and shook his head. 'So odd that he should have forgotten Henry James. The most frightening scene ever written . . . when the spirit of Quint comes to the window in *The Turn of the Screw*. And even odder that he should have said nothing about dictators and windows. They lean out of them on every possible occasion, unfortunately never quite far enough. You must be photographed from a window yourself, one day. It would be excellent publicity.'

'Thank you, Marius.'

'I must be going.' He paused and looked around him, first at the gaping windows and then out into the cluttered corridor. 'Do you know your Thomas Gray?'

'Only the "Elegy".'

'Not his best poem. You should read "A Long Story".

There's a couplet in it which is a perfect description of what our Mr. Stebbing seems to have aimed at when he was trying to spoil this house:

> Rich windows that exclude the light
> And passages that lead to nothing.'

He strolled away down one of these passages. There was the rattling of a door, a scrunching of rubble, an amiable oath, and he was gone.

But no. A moment later he was back again. He pushed his head through the door, which as usual he had omitted to close.

'I felt I should tell you that I had left the door open *deliberately*.'

'There was no need to bother, Marius. It's only because of the rubble on the floor.'

'I don't think you understand. Do you remember what Pascal said about the troubles of mankind?'

'He said so much that . . .'

'But the one *final* thing?' he interrupted. The one thing *everybody* knows? The one thing they put on *Christmas* cards?'

'I don't read what they put on Christmas cards.'

'You make a great mistake. Pascal said that all the troubles of mankind arose from one simple fact . . . that mankind would never sit down quietly in one room.'

'There's a lot to be said for that.'

'There is indeed. But Pascal omitted one quite vital fact. He should have added . . . *with the door open*.'

'Why?'

'I despair of you. Why? Because the abolition of locks and keys would be the greatest revolution that had ever occurred in the history of civilization. Think of it! At a single stroke you would wipe the insurance companies off the map. You would make the job of Governor of the Bank of England a ridiculous sinecure. You would destroy the capitalist system.'

'Do you *want* to destroy the capitalist system?'

'Not in the least. The capitalists, yes. But not the system. Have I said anything to suggest that I wanted to do so?'

'I'm not quite sure. You have said so much that I am rather confused.'

He smiled and drew his arm through mine. 'You must forgive me. It's that cocktail of yours.'

We walked down the steps and out into the lane. The wind was still rising, and it was nearly dark. Marius turned and stared at the old house.

'Well, whatever else I may have said, there is only one word to remember – Fenestralia. Or in this case, fenestration. Look at your house. Do you know why it makes me feel angry?'

'Angry?'

'Yes. Very angry indeed. Because you have done so many things to it, and they are all absolutely right, but you have not done the most important thing of all. You've torn down that hideous bay, you've demolished the loggia, you've ripped off half a dozen drain pipes, you've banished the Edwardian railings. But you've not brought it back to life.'

'Why?'

'Why?' He gripped my arm more tightly. 'My dear fellow, look at the windows!'

And then, at last, I saw what he meant. It was, of course, inexcusable that I had not realized it before, but there had been so many other things to do, so many obvious horrors to tackle, apart from the sheer business of living.

The windows were dead. They were blank, square sheets of glass that stared out into the lane with sightless eyes. It was Mr. Stebbing, needless to say, who had been responsible for this outrage. He had torn out the delicate Georgian panes of squared glass which, as I ought to have known, were absolutely essential to the Georgian pattern – and replaced them by these bleak, single sheets. It was as drastic and inexcusable an operation as cutting out the eyes of a portrait.

So *that* was what had been worrying me all these months . . . that was what had been filling me with this vague disquiet.

'Thank you, Marius,' I said. 'As usual, you win.'

He bowed and shook me by the hand. 'My next lecture, I trust,' he said, 'will be somewhat less expensive.' With which he wandered away.

Indeed I hope so, I thought, as I went back to the house. The windows must be changed at once . . . at least a dozen of them. What it would all cost, with the new glass, and the 'making good', and the rain coming in on the new paint, and the general uproar and confusion, I simply dared not think. As for what Gaskin would say. . . .

I went in to finish my cocktail; in the excitement of these affairs I had forgotten to drink it. Then I went in to inform Gaskin. Over that scene, perhaps, it would be wise to draw a veil.

§ I I I

That first winter, then, might be called the Winter of the Windows. It was a winter of considerable discontent for a number of people, including the cats, who retreated further and further into the great open fireplace as the draughts swept through the house. Indeed, they took to sleeping in the fireplace at night, so that when you met them in the morning their noses were powdered with wood-ash, and when you stroked them they emitted clouds of dust.

But it was a winter of great content for me. As each blank pane was removed, to be replaced by its delicate squared counterpart, the house seemed to open another eye, and to stare with delight on the garden which had so long been denied to it. Every view was transformed; I used to wander upstairs and down, from the attics to the cellars, peering out in all weathers. It would be hard to say when this window-gazing was most delectable. Maybe when the rain was beating on them, so that their landscapes were laden with tears. Or when the frost had traced on them its miraculous fernery, so that you saw the bare branches outside through a curtain of silver lace. Or late at night, when the rooms were dark, and the curtains were undrawn, and the panes were black as jet. You had to go very close up to the windows then, and press your nose against the glass before you could see the first glimmer of the snowdrops in the bed outside the drawing-room.

Best of all, perhaps, I liked the dormer windows in the roof, which were the last to be transformed. Their view was cramped and restricted – just a stretch of roof and a patch of sky and a waving branch of lime tree, stretching up to greet you; but there was something very exciting in being so high up, so remote, among the chimney-tops, and in feeling that all this strange collection of bricks and mortar and slates and pipes and beams and glass – all this great pile of material, that had been challenging the seasons for nearly two centuries, actually belonged to *you*. And that it belonged to you simply and solely because you had written a number of words on a number of sheets of paper. At times it seemed almost unfair that anything so solid and enduring should have been given to you in exchange for anything so flimsy and ephemeral. Then, when you remembered the number of words that you had written it did not seem unfair at all. It seemed very right and proper. The wind, wailing round the roof, up there under the beams in the dust and the emptiness, seemed to echo your sentiments.

But there is one window at Merry Hall which means more to me than any of the others—a certain window in the music-room. Since its construction was directly due to the burglary, this is perhaps the right moment to tell you about it.

Which brings me, with a bump, to the water-closet.

If your story includes, as one of its essential dramatic properties, a water-closet, it is better to get it over and done with, and to say it outright. After all, we live in an age of plain-speaking. The great majority of modern American novels, for example, are largely concerned with water-closets. Indeed, one is forced to the conclusion that they have often been inspired by water-closets, and composed in them. My music-room water-closet has no sinister significance at all; it is merely an architectural feature to which I am obliged to refer. I cannot refer to it as the Thing. That would be distracting. Nor can I transform it into a Gazebo. Nor drop whimsical little hints about washing the hands. It must just be a plain water-closet.

So let us draw a plan.

This is the far end of the music-room . . . the end, that is to say, of the house . . . in the week after the burglary.

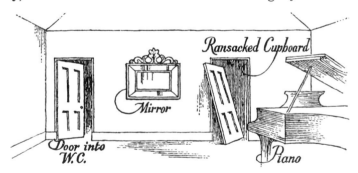

The obvious thing to do, I suppose, would have been to restore the door of the cupboard, get another safe, to buy at least one feeble nine-carat gold cigarette case, and pretend that nothing had happened.

But I didn't feel at all in that mood. I was 'off' gold cigarette cases. I was 'off' safes, too. One could have too much of this darned thing called 'security'. It is a deadening word –

drab and passive. I did not feel all that drab, nor all that passive.

So one afternoon I went in and tore off the door. I was confronted by a deep recess – the late cupboard. The recess suggested a window. But how could one have a window that looked out on to a toolshed? By frosting it? But wouldn't plain frosted glass look rather pointless? Yes, it would. So why not frame the window with a grille – a really beautiful grille in the most delicate ironwork of the eighteenth century? And why not get Mr. Young to light it up from behind? And . . . oh dear . . . what would Gaskin say?

To hell with it! There should be a window. There should be a grille. There should be a light behind it. And it would all be of entrancing beauty. It would all be so beautiful, indeed, that the eye would be automatically drawn to the right, leaving the Gazebo to lurk in obscurity. As Gazebos should.

As soon as the great decision was made, I hurried out, jumped into the car, and shot down the lane, bound for Mr. Crowther's at Isleworth. I have already referred to Mr. Crowther's unique establishment, in a previous volume,[1] so we need not go into all that again. It is enough to say that it is a cluster of fantastic gardens, filled with the most remarkable collection of antiquities that can ever have been gathered together in this world – avenues of statues, sundials, gates, pineapples, nymphs and fountains – multitudes of urns, vases, plaques, fanlights, cherubs, dolphins, garden seats and leaden peacocks – all jostling each other in a mad and glorious confusion in the shadow of immense mulberry trees and in a tangle of white roses and gnarled wistaria. It is hard to believe that this dream-like miscellany is a place of commerce, especially as one may wander through its enchanted groves for hours without meeting anybody who shows the least inclination to sell you anything. Such, however, it is . . . and

[1] *Merry Hall.*

on this occasion I was quite determined that somebody should sell me an iron grille.

The ironwork at Crowther's lies in an old courtyard, piled round and about the trunks of the aforesaid mulberry trees. There is enough of it to sink a battleship and it is all beautiful. One could prowl for hours through piles of ancient gates and grilles and chains and fire-backs. In this case I literally stumbled on what I wanted. It lay on the ground, with the weeds climbing through it. It was of impeccable elegance – a square of wrought iron enclosing a design of the most delicate scrolls and leaves and flourishes, with the profiles of two satyrs standing out, bold and black, in the centre. It was not in very good repair; it would need quite a lot doing to it; and if I had been a man of business I should obviously have pointed this out to the old salesman who eventually drifted out from the shadow of the mulberry trees. Instead, I found myself saying to him that it was really too beautiful, and he clasped his hands and sighed and said yes it was, and I asked him about repairing it, and he bent down and touched it gently and affectionately, and said that one could take a scroll from the back and put it in the front, and hammer out a rose that had been misshapen. And we both became so enraptured by the whole transaction that when I left I found that I had bought it without either asking the price or giving the old man my address. Which is how business, I think, should always be conducted.

So that was the most beautiful window of all, in this Winter of the Windows. When I am dead, I do hope that no one will do away with it. It would be too distressing if some frightful man – probably an author – were to buy the house, and stalk into the music-room, and stare at the window and feel about it as I felt about Mr. Stebbing's Spero Meliora. I don't see how he *could* feel about it that way, for every curve of the design of my window was obviously moulded with love, and the two satyrs are really the nicest creatures, with dispositions as engaging as their profiles. But perhaps the author might not understand that. Perhaps he might be anti-satyr, anti everything that I love. It is all most agitating. It 'only goes to show' – as Gaskin would say – that one should not cross one's bridges before they have been reached. In other words, that one should not worry about the Styx before one has had at least a tentative introduction to Charon.

CHAPTER FOUR

A PIECE OF GLASS

IT is high time that we made the tour of the house. We shall be wandering about it together, for some time to come, and it will be a bore for you if you do not know your way around.

Let us begin at the beginning, as though we had just arrived to pay a call.

Merry Hall is a small square Georgian box of a building, to which two extensions were added some fifty years ago, one at the side and one at the back. The side extension – it really cannot be called a 'wing', because that would be altogether too grand – consists of the kitchen, which is vast, and Gaskin's premises, which are pretty extensive. The back extension consists entirely of the music-room.

Pause for breath. If you are as bad as I am at grasping this sort of description, you will already be feeling dizzy. So let us repeat – the main Georgian box, the block at the side, and the big music-room at the back.

The house stands in a quiet lane, with a twelve-acre field

across the road. In this field, at times, an exceptionally female cow appears, glares at my front door, and makes noises like a fog-horn. This is the occasion for a sharp interchange of notes between myself and Mrs. Maples, the owner of the farm where the cow belongs. The cow is then led off to make noises in another field.

You walk across a tiny lawn, up a flight of steps, and, I hope, you pause to admire the doorway. It is, I think, a perfect late Georgian doorway, with two slender wooden pillars on each side, an arch, and a fanlight.

You pass through the front door into a short corridor, at the end of which is a small hall, from which a pretty staircase runs up to the first floor. It is all very white and light and airy, in these days – the corridor invites you, and the staircase beckons you to come and see where it leads. When I first arrived it was dark and gloomy, even on the sunniest day, with a wallpaper of orange and magenta, and the Spero Meliora window casting its dim and aqueous shadows over the walls. You were almost afraid to walk up the staircase, because you felt certain that some awful creature would be lurking at the top, somebody like a sort of insane dentist, waiting to spring.

Here we are then, standing at the bottom of the staircase. So far so good.

Now let us turn our heads to the right. Here is a door, and if we were to open it we should step into the drawing-room, which is the biggest room in the house, and contains most of its modest treasures – the Canaletto . . . ('school of'!) – the William and Mary chairs – the Hepplewhite settee – the Sheraton sofa-table – the Chippendale mirror – and various other things that I shall probably talk about so often that you will feel like throwing them out of the window.

But don't let's go into the drawing-room just yet; let's keep it for a little while.

Instead – still standing at the bottom of the staircase – let us look to the left. Here there is another door, which gives access to the dining-room. If we were to open it I think you would like what you saw inside, for it is all white and daffodil yellow, with some very pretty Regency chairs, and long curtains of faded yellow velvet. There are crystal lustres on the walls, which give a rainbow magic to the room when the sun is setting. Sometimes in the evening the coloured lights that sparkle from these prisms are so enchanting that I sit down and watch them, in the silence, entirely forgetting what I have come in for. Once, I remember, they shone on to a bowl of white roses, so that the petals were flecked with violet, and the leaves were specked with blue, and there were yellow shadows in the water.

But let the dining-room wait, and let us walk straight ahead into what we will call the Inner Hall. It sounds rather grand, but it is really quite modest. Its main feature is a small fireplace, with a mantelpiece of unpolished pine, which is reputed – by me! – to have been carved by Grinling Gibbons. Over this mantelpiece hangs one of the four good pictures I possess, a landscape by Patrick Nasmyth, who was a contemporary of Constable, and sometimes, I think, his equal.

§ 11

We are more than half way through, and the rest is very plain sailing, so I hope you can bear this tedious stuff for a few moments more.

We can ignore the door ahead, into the kitchen, and the door next to it, which hides the nose-powdering department, and go straight through to the conservatory, which leads to the music-room.

The conservatory is really something. (The word 'conservatory', which I rather like, is used to distinguish it from the big greenhouse, which is in the kitchen garden.) The dead hand of Mr. Stebbing hung heavy over this conservatory when I first arrived. With devilish ingenuity he had contrived that the main drain from upstairs should be let through the roof, like a sort of pillar, so that it was apt to stun all who passed that way. At crucial moments it sent out embarrassing gurgles and hisses, usually when one was showing people the geraniums. This drain has now been diverted, and bricked up with a square column, painted white. In summer it is covered with a riot of pale blue plumbago.

The removal of the drain was one of the few things which Miss Emily, from delicacy rather than from desire, was unable to deplore. When she first stepped into the conservatory on her way to the music-room she paused, flinched, and exclaimed:

'Dear me . . . more changes! Now let me see, what have we done *here?*'

I could not think of any polite way of saying that I had removed the main drain from the upstairs lavatory, so I ignored the question.

'Yes . . . what *have* we done?' demanded Our Rose, who was standing by her side.

Miss Emily suddenly realized that her question was embarrassing. 'Something structural, dear,' she murmured.

'Yes, but *what?*'

Miss Emily glared at her. '*Structural*, dear,' she repeated.

'But that might mean anything. . . .'

'Quite, dear,' snapped Miss Emily. 'It might.' With which she passed through to the music-room, where in a moment we will follow her.

But first, may we pause for a moment in this little glass corridor, to note what we may expect to see in it? After all, it is a very vital part of the house; it links the old with the new, by a chain of flowers. It is one of Oldfield's most sacred preserves; every morning, on the stroke of nine, his white head may be seen bending over the shelves of geraniums, tapping the pots to see if they are dry enough to need watering.

'How can you tell, just by tapping?' I once asked him.

His one good eye regarded me with some scorn. 'You can tell by t'sound' he said. He tapped one of the pots. 'That's dry.' He tapped another. 'That could do with a drop.' And another. 'That's not needing any.'

'They all sound just the same, to me.'

He did not comment on this pitiable statement. He had noticed that the watering can was empty. He gave me a reproachful look. 'I see you've been using my water to fill t'vases again.'

'I'm so sorry, Oldfield. I meant to fill up the can again last night. I'll get you a drop of warm from the kitchen.'

'T'isn't the same. Not as if it had stood here all night. Still, t'is better than cold. If there's one thing makes geraniums spalch off, t'is cold water.'

'Spalch' is one of several new words which Oldfield has added to my vocabulary. It is not in the Oxford Dictionary, but it is a good old word, still current in Lancashire, which means to die back, to wither prematurely.

We must not linger here too long, talking to Oldfield, but first I must justify my claim that the conservatory is 'really something'. Perhaps I can describe it most vividly by saying that this is the place where women, as soon as they step into it, exclaim with a sharp 'Oh!' Sometimes this is varied by 'Oh no!' or 'Oh really!' This sounds as though they had been pounced on from behind, and subjected to nippings, but this is not why they cry out. It is because there is always some sort of display which justifies the exclamation. In winter there is a bank of snow-white chrysanthemums on which I have trained a spot-light, to heighten the illusion of a ballet. In spring there is a glorious tumble of schizanthus, which I prefer to call by its common name – 'Poor Man's Orchid'. For indeed, no show of orchids could rival the rich purples and mauves and pinks and crimsons of this deliciously overdressed creature. In the summer, the sprays of plumbago dance right up to the roof, their pale blue blossom glimmering against the deeper blue of the sky.

And throughout the whole year there are geraniums, which to me are a sort of 'test flower', for the long experience has taught me that people who do not like geraniums have something morally unsound about them. Sooner or later you will find them out; you will discover that they drink, or steal books, or speak sharply to cats. Never trust a man or a woman who is not passionately devoted to geraniums. But then, of course, all displays of geraniums are not as exciting as mine, where the plain scarlet is jostled by the double magenta, which fights shrilly with the giant salmon, surrounded by a medley of apple-blossoms, and deep pinks, and pure whites, all wrapped around in the subtle scent of the fragrant leaves.

There is one last, purely personal, reason why I love the conservatory. It is because of the rain on the roof. It is of all sounds the most evocative. If you leave the door slightly ajar, when you are sitting by the fire in the music-room on a winter night, the sound of the falling rain is like music, which mingles with the hiss of the logs and the sigh of the pines outside. On stormy days in spring, when the sky is like a blue carpet over which a giant has suddenly thrown a bucket of black ink, and when the rain comes down with the sweep of a silver sword, the uproar on the roof is almost terrifying—the cats rush away and crouch on the staircase, you wonder how the frail glass can withstand so fierce an assault.

Now, at last, we can enter the music-room, which will be for the moment the end of our journey, for you cannot wish to be dragged through seven upstairs bedrooms, to say nothing of a rabbit-warren of attics and outbuildings.

As we enter it, we shall see. . . .

But no. I don't want you to see it as it is today. I want you to see it as it was in the beginning, fresh from the hands of that evil genius, Mr. Stebbing.

It is a large room, with a high ceiling, and wide windows facing East and South, through which one catches a perpetual play of dancing branches. Anybody with the least sense of decency would immediately realize that here was a room that was created for music – for making music and for listening to it, for rushing into, in winter, and striking furious chords, for creeping into, on summer nights, and putting down the soft pedal, and imagining – not very successfully – that one is the reincarnation of Debussy. If your interest is exclusively in ball games, you will not be allured by the picture this evokes. But if you do not mind making an idiot of yourself, in the name of Chopin and Mozart, you may perhaps sympathize.

The late Mr. Stebbing's interests *were*, very largely, in ball games, apart from his exercise on the pianola, where, as you may remember, he played Liszt for the benefit of his intestines. (Even that, when one comes to think of it, might be described as a dim sort of ball game.) Therefore the late Mr. Stebbing had transformed this potential chamber of enchantment into that silliest of all things, a billiards-room. We are all, I hope, agreed that there is nothing whatever to be said for billiards. It is a nasty invention that causes its victims to crouch, for hours on end, in attitudes which nobody could describe as decorative.

My first task, therefore, was to do something to this room, which should proclaim, instantly and dramatically, that whatever else people might use it for, they would not use it for billiards.

Which brings us to the blue chandelier.

§ I I I

But before we can come to the blue chandelier, and stand under it, and gaze up at it, and step away from it, and turn on the lights to watch it sparkle in one shade, and turn them off to watch it sparkle in another – before we can indulge in

66

these alluring pastimes, over which at least an hour might be spent with the greatest profit – I must explain how it was that I came to buy it at all.

In the beginning, when we first moved into Merry Hall, I had so little furniture that it was funny. I ought to have had a great deal, but everything was blown up during the war. So that when the furniture van eventually drew up at the front door, my possessions looked sadly meagre as they were brought into the light of day. They were, to be precise. . . .

A Steinway piano.

Three beds.

A few wheel-back chairs.

Several electric fires, of the wrong voltage.

A Queen Anne chafing dish.

A revolving Regency bedside book-table, that revolved so fast that it shot all the books out of it, like bullets.

An Empire settee.

A number of very nasty velvet cushions, triangular in shape, edged with gold brocade.

A gigantic Victorian dinner service, which I had bought in a moment of madness. It had soup tureens the size of cradles. Every piece was monogrammed A. V. A., so I had to invent a great-aunt called Augustine Victoria Alington, who was supposed to have left it to me.

A minimum of kitchen things, a minimum of sheets and blankets, and about a thousand books.

Obviously, in these circumstances, one had to do something about it, and I did what most people would have done – I bought junk. That is to say, I fitted the music-room with blue felt, and bought a set of cane garden chairs. For the drawing-room I got a worm-eaten walnut William and Mary bureau, which was rather more William than Mary, and some dark red curtains. In front of this I placed the Empire settee, which might have looked all right if Madame Recamier had been lying on it, straining her dorsal muscles and smirking at posterity. As it was it looked lost, and it swore at William and Mary.

For the rest, it was a question of going round the cheaper antique shops in Chelsea and Fulham, and buying bits of rubbish that would do 'until we get something better'.

It was at this stage of the proceedings that Bob came back into my life.

Some of my readers will have met Bob before.[1] He it was who came down with me to 'vet' the house before I bought it, and he it was who prophesied disaster, bankruptcy and the imminent decease of Gaskin through over-work. I hope you may like to meet him again, as he steps out of an exquisite new Daimler coupé, stands on the steps, and sniffs the country air. In case you have forgotten what he looks like, let us note that he is about forty, with prematurely grey hair, large black eyes that flicker between melancholy and malice, and restless hands. In moments of emotion – which with him are frequent – he dives into his pocket, and produces from it a singular assortment of golden objects hanging on to the end of a chain . . . a gold lighter, a gold latch-key, a gold champagne stick, a gold compass, and several golden charms. This collection is rattled, with some vehemence, to give point to his remarks.

Bob is very rich, and very generous. Unlike some of the members of his race, he spends much of his time laughing at himself.

'What a lovely new car, Bob.'

A deep sigh, and a faint rattle of chains. '*How* one manages, my dear, on a mere *pittance*, I do *not* know.' And then, turning to George, his chauffeur . . . 'George . . . *chives*.'

'Yes, sir.'

'You don't mind, Beverley my dear? There isn't a chive in London. I've *scoured* the entire city. So I thought if Oldfield could give me the *teeniest* clump. . . .'

[1] In *Merry Hall* (Cape).

68

'But of course, Bob.'

'And George. . . .'

'Yes, sir?'

'Perhaps Oldfield could put them in a *pot*. And then they will keep on growing, and we can have them for weeks.'

'Yes, sir.'

'So kind of you, Beverley my dear. My cook will be enchanted. She's been nearly going off her head about chives. And George. . . .'

'Yes, sir?'

'Perhaps you would ask Oldfield to give them a spot of *water*. And when you put them in the car, don't put them on the seat. And George. . . .'

'Yes, sir?'

Here there is a rattle of chains, and Bob hands to George a present for Oldfield, which is worth a great deal more than any amount of chives. By the end of the day, the pot of chives will have been joined by a bunch of mint . . . ('not a *sprig* of mint in London, my dear') . . . and a small bundle of tarragon.

The business of the chives completed, Bob heaves another sigh, and gazes around him.

'It all looks wonderfully tidy,' he observes, in tones of some distress. 'Does Oldfield still do it all?'

'Yes.'

'Of course, he'll kill himself one of these days.'

'He seems to be taking a long time about it.'

'Did he spray all these roses?'

'As a matter of fact, they haven't been sprayed at all.'

'That, my dear Beverley, I can *not* be expected to believe.' A distinct rattle of chains. 'When I had *my* garden, with *seven* gardeners, I had every sort of blight except locusts, and that was in *spite* of the fact that they were sprayed from morning till night. I even tried to hire a helicopter. Your roses *must* have been sprayed. Perhaps the odd man did them?'

'I haven't had an odd man for weeks.'

'Then all I can say is that it makes me feel quite sick. I had an entire *ballet* of odd men. And not a chive could they grow. Not one. As for asparagus . . . I suppose you'll tell me you've got cartloads of asparagus?'

'I've got quite a lot.'

Bob gives me a look which, from anybody but an old friend, would be regarded as murderous. 'I hope we're having some of it for luncheon?'

'We are.'

Slightly mollified, he drifts inside.

It may easily be imagined that in these earliest days – the junk-buying period – Bob had a great deal to say. Indeed it was through him that the word 'junk', as applied to my possessions, first came into my mind, and through him that I was first shamed into a desire for better things. Which is another way, I suppose, of saying that he stirred in me the beginnings of taste.

Let me recall a typical moment, about six months after we had moved in, when Bob launched his first attack on my junk-buying proclivities. He strutted round the house, very swiftly, pausing before each object, rattling his chains at it, and apostrophizing it. Thus:

'Riddled with worm, my dear. And you know what happens when you get *worm*. . . .'

'Its bottom has nothing to do with its top, my dear. And the railing is bogus. . . .'

'No, my dear, it is *not* ormulu. It is brass. And one of its legs is missing. . . .'

I tried to defend myself by pointing out that I had to have some furniture, and that I could not afford to buy the sort of thing that I should have liked. He waved these considerations aside with the utmost disdain.

'My dear Beverley, it is all *junk*. And you know it.'

'Perhaps I do, Bob. But . . .'

'*Never* buy junk. It never pays.'

'I'm sure it doesn't, Bob. But . . .'

'There are no "buts" about it. Look at these absurd chairs!' He pointed to the six cane chairs which, apart from the piano, formed almost the sole furniture of the music-room. 'How much did you pay for them?'

'I think they were eight pounds each.'

'Eight pounds each!' He addressed this remark, in outraged accents, to the ceiling. 'Eight pounds! I really despair of you, my dear Beverley. Do you realize that you have paid nearly fifty pounds for those chairs?'

'In actual fact, I haven't paid for them at all, as yet.'

He ignored this quibble. 'Nearly fifty pounds. And if you wanted to sell them again . . .'

'I have no desire to sell them again . . .'

'. . . You would get, at the *most*, twenty pounds!'

He paused and glared at me, in order to allow the full horror of this information to sink in.

'Now if you had bought *one* chair, or some delicious *objet*, like that ormulu pineapple I brought back from Copenhagen . . .'

'But Bob . . .'

'Have you *seen* my ormulu pineapple?'

I had indeed seen it, and very elegant it looked, especially since he had placed it on a Louis XV buhl table for which he had paid eight hundred pounds. But, as I should have liked to explain, one could not *sit* on ormulu pineapples, unless one was a person of the most eccentric tastes. Nor could more than one person sit on one chair.

'Do you know how much I *paid* for my ormulu pineapple?' he continued, in rising tones. 'Thirty pounds! And I could sell it tomorrow for three hundred! In fact, if I showed it to that *fiend* . . .'(Here he named a mutual acquaintance, who was also a collector) . . . 'I could probably get five hundred. Not that I should let her have even a *peek* at it. There are limits.'

He sank down on the sofa, and shook his head sadly at my folly in refraining from buying ormulu pineapples.

'Of course' he admitted grudgingly, 'this room is quite pretty – if you don't look at it too closely.'

'Thank you, Bob.'

'But, my dear Beverley – why *felt?*'

'Well Bob . . .'

'You know what *happens* to felt?'

(He made this remark sound extraordinarily sinister, as though he were about to tell me that it came out in some ghastly fungus, or got up off the floor and walked about in the night in a sort of blue mist.)

'No. What?'

'Everything.' He shook his head gloomily, and bent forward to examine it. 'Yes. It's happening already. All the pile is wearing off. In three years' time it will be a *rag*.'

'But in three years' time I may have written a best-seller, and Hollywood will buy it, and . . .'

'And you will get fourpence-halfpenny by the time the income-tax people have finished with it. Did I tell you about *my* income-tax? No? Well I won't. It would make you sick. Have you met Mr. Pontremoli?'

'No. Does he do things with income tax?'

A fierce rattle of chains greeted this remark. 'Mr. Pontremoli sells carpets.'

'Oh! Are they very expensive?'

'No. They cost a lot of money, but they are *not* expensive. How much did you pay for this felt?'

'About a hundred pounds.'

'I thought so! And if you were to try to sell it tomorrow . . .'

'But Bob, why do you keep on assuming that I want to sell everything tomorrow?'

'Tomorrow,' he repeated, 'you would be lucky to get fifty. Whereas if you had gone to Mr. Pontremoli you could have got a piece of Queen Anne needlework that was so exquisite that you'd want to hang it on the wall.'

'That would hardly help to carpet the floor.'

'Of course, if you look at everything like *that* . . .' He finished the remark with a positive tattoo of chain-rattling.

In the days ahead, it was destined that I was to pay a visit, with Bob, to Mr. Pontremoli, and not only to pay a visit but to purchase a Bokhara carpet, at such a staggering price that I felt quite dizzy while I was driving it home in the car. It was one of the best investments I ever made, and 'if I were to sell it tomorrow' . . . But I hope I never will.

§ I V

And now at last, the blue chandelier, or you will be beginning to think that I invented it.

Bob's visit had somewhat depressed me. When he had departed, surrounded by chives, mint and tarragon, I wandered back into the music-room and looked around me. It was all a lot of nothing. Just the piano, and the blue felt, and those idiotic cane chairs. If the *Woman's Own* came down and took photographs, as they threatened to do, it would need a great deal of trick lighting to avoid the impression that the bailiffs had been in. And a lot of clever captions, which I should have to write myself. 'STARK SIMPLICITY IS THE KEYNOTE OF THIS POPULAR AUTHOR'S RETREAT.' It would have to be on those lines. We could move up one of the cane chairs, and drape a sheet over it, and obscure the foreground with a bowl of roses, and try to persuade 'One' to sit on the piano and gaze at me, with the Empire bedside table in the background. That would do for the music-room. But what about the drawing-room? That would have to be 'ANTIQUE AND MODERN BLEND IN HAPPY HARMONY IN AUTHOR'S GEORGIAN MANSION'. In other words, the Regency settee would have to be pushed into the foreground, with another of the cane chairs beside it, camouflaged with a different sheet; and perhaps we should be able to persuade 'One' to sit on it again, if he had not been driven into a state of advanced hysteria by the flashlights. Then I could drape myself on the settee, and gaze, with frenzied interest, at the William and Mary cupboard, hoping that when the photograph was published it would not betray the fact that it was riddled with worm.

That was really all I had to offer, in the furniture line, to the three million readers of *Woman's Own*, unless I went upstairs and jumped into bed. But that would mean that the Empire bedside table would have to be dragged into prominence again, and by then people would be beginning to get rather sick of it. Besides, I had not even got a bed-head. Just a plain bed, with its back to a white wall. Indeed, my bedroom was about as glamorous as a sergeant's hut, which suited me very well, but might not appeal to the photographers.

No. Something must be done.

I sat down heavily in a cane chair. I closed my eyes. And suddenly I saw a flash of blue.

It was not a twinge of rheumatism. Nor was it a psychic manifestation. It was just a memory . . . a memory of a grey November day, some six months before, when I had been motoring through a little village on the upper reaches of the Thames. The sky had been leaden, the river a sheet of steel, and the light was fading fast. I had turned my head to look at a signpost, and there – flashing past – was a window, and in the window a glint of blue. Real Mediterranean blue – the authentic glitter, the unearthly magic.

I put on the brakes and got out. Inside the shop there was a little man like a bat, standing under a blue chandelier. He was so small and so dark and so twisted that you felt he had just dropped down out of some mysterious nest which he had woven in the blue glass branches. But there was nothing in the least exotic about his idea of business. When I asked him the price of the chandelier he named an outrageous figure.

I tried not to look too disappointed. I also tried not to gaze too hungrily at the blue miracle above me. For it really was

74

a miracle. It was a large chandelier, but so delicate in design that it hung as lightly as a cluster of floating bubbles. It was presumably Venetian, and its date was about 1830. But what really mattered was the brilliance and variety of its colour. It had the innocent blue of harebells and the subtle blue of

sapphires; in its twisted leaves and chains there were the shadows of gentians and the clear eyes of speedwells; there were the wings of butterflies and the petals of delphiniums; there were deep waters and spring skies, and every blue that God ever gave to us, when He painted this wonderful world.

I decided there and then that I must have it, if it was still there. It had suddenly become a necessity. Anything that could haunt one like that, through all these months, was obviously destined to play a part in one's life.

I will not describe the rush to the garage, the frenzied

drive through the country roads to get to the shop before closing time, the discovery of the little man, standing in exactly the same position as he had been standing before – and my sense of triumph when I beat him down from guineas to pounds. It is enough to say that within the hour it was mine, and on the following day it was delivered to Merry Hall.

§ V

There are a thousand definitions of Life, but I cannot recall that I have ever seen the most obvious one of all, namely, that life is light. 'Let there be Light,' said the Lord Our God, when the world was only an idea, still lingering in the ancient darkness. 'Let there be *Light*' – not 'Let there be *Life*'. Maybe, to the Lord Our God, the two words were synonymous. But since He was, and is, a poet, He chose the more musical phrase, the phrase that illuminated the whole universe of His creation, like the sun rising on an empty stage.

I have thought of these things very often, as a gardener, when wandering about, choosing a place to plant things, finding the right degree of shade for the camellias, so that the morning sun will not strike them after a frosty night, to turn their petals brown . . . contriving that the little winter daphnes shall have their roots in the shade and their heads in the sun . . . cutting back the branches of a mock orange so that the sun may shine its fiercest on the ivy geraniums that hang from the terra-cotta bowls outside the music-roon. Ivy geraniums cannot have too much sun, as you will realize if you have seen them rioting over the cliffs above the magic bay of Villefranche. Yes, light in a garden is a quarter of the battle. Another quarter is the soil of the garden. A third quarter is the skill and care of the gardener. The fourth quarter is luck. Indeed, one might say that these were the four L's of gardening, in the following order of importance:

Loam
Light
Love
Luck

As it is in a garden, so it is in a house. Therefore, if you ever want to think of Merry Hall, as I hope you sometimes may, you must think first of this sparkling crystal flower, floating from the high ceiling of the music-room. And you must think of it not merely as a piece of decoration, but as something that lives, something with a thousand moods, which it echoes from the life of the garden outside. On a clear winter morning, after a heavy snowfall, when the music-room is flooded with icy sunlight, it seems to deepen in colour, so that it hangs like a cluster of miraculous, luminous grapes. On summer nights, when the moonlight is stealing through the branches of the lime tree, so gently, so softly, as though it were afraid of waking the sleeping leaves, the chandelier takes to itself a tinge of green. . . If you come down to visit it, in the dead of night, you see that there are emeralds among the sapphires, and that the azure stem has been interlaced with jade. There are times, too, when the room is noisy and full of people, and very much alive with the light of the candles and the darting flames of the log fire, that the chandelier has a golden sheen, the chains and the flowers seem moulded of precious metal.

So there we are. That is the true foundation of the house that this particular Jack built. A bubble of glass. Not a very solid one, you may say. But perhaps it may endure as long as some of the others.

CHAPTER FIVE

N . W . H .

THIS book was intended as a Landscape with Figures, but
so far the figures have been crowded out.

True, Gaskin has been here and there with cocktails
on a tray – a very cracked and shabby tray, too, which
reminds me that the house is still largely unfurnished.
Marius has drifted along, too seldom for my liking, since he
never fails to teach me something. Miss Emily and Our Rose
have made occasional appearances – again too seldom. For
though they drive me into frenzies of irritation, they do at
least stimulate me to action. One day I shall be so maddened
by Our Rose's flower decorations that I shall do something
which will cause what is known as a Breach in Our Relationship. I shall take a large sponge and stuff it with gentians and
serve it up to her for dinner on a plate. The agony of it is
that she will probably adore it.

Who else? Well – Bob paid us a visit, rattled his golden
chains, and disappeared in an aura of chives and mint. And
of course, there has always been Oldfield. Indeed, you
cannot imagine Merry Hall without him. Every time you
look out of the window he is there, walking across the lawn
with a basket of vegetables, trailing off to the orchard with a
ladder over his shoulder, double-digging the new border by

the south wall, and generally doing far more work than he ought to do, even if he were half his age.

But now, several new figures begin to move into the landscape. They are very real figures to me, and I hope they may also seem so to you. So let me try to paint them clearly, as they step on to the green lawn, with the old house in the background, and 'One' and 'Four' asleep on the steps.

Let us begin with Miss Mint, for until we have met her we cannot understand the mysterious letters at the head of our chapter.

§ 11

Whenever I think of Miss Mint, I think of these three letters.

However long you were to wrack your brains, you would not guess what they stand for, so I will tell you right away. They mean . . .

NOTHING WRONG HERE

N.W.H. appears, almost invariably, in the top left-hand corner of the envelopes of the letters which Miss Mint writes to her friends, and I have often thought that they hold the key to her endearing but somewhat eccentric character. She herself – she had a very unhappy childhood – is so timid, so beset with nameless fears and alarms, that the arrival of any sort of communication fills her with foreboding. The postman whistling down the lane is a figure of approaching doom, and if he pauses at her cottage, and drops a letter through her door, it is several minutes before she can summon up enough courage to open it.

It has never occurred to Miss Mint that others do not share her misgivings, and since she has infinite kindness and consideration, she has contrived this device to set their minds at ease. 'I do wish that everybody would adopt it,' she once said to me. 'It is so very simple, and saves so much suspense.'

'It might be rather complicated,' I suggested. 'Particularly with business letters.'

'Surely even business firms are human?'

'What about the income tax people? If *they* put N.W.H. on their envelopes it might sound rather ironic.'

Miss Mint sighed. Yes, she said. She supposed it would. It was all very difficult.

Once I received a letter from Miss Mint on which the mystic symbols were missing. My heart gave a painful leap; I feared the worst. But no, the letter was only to ask me to tea on the following Tuesday, and to tell me that her Morning Glories, which she thought were all blue, had come up mixed. This could hardly be construed as a major disaster, and I guessed that Miss Mint, for once in a way, had forgotten. My surmise was correct, for later in the morning another note was found on the mat, with N.W.H. in extra large letters, to reassure me that there had, in fact, been 'nothing wrong'. She has never forgotten again.

Miss Mint came into our lives in my third year at Merry Hall, and since it was Marius who introduced her, we were all disposed to feel kindly towards her, even if she herself had not been such an oddly lovable little creature. She was short and grey and mousey, and though there was nothing studied about her appearance, she called to mind the ladies of Cranford. They would hardly have turned their heads if they had met her walking down their immortal High Street, and they would have welcomed her at their candle-lit parties.

It was at a candle-lit party that I met her myself – a tea-party which Marius gave for her in his house in the woods of Great Lacing. This house is a white, rambling building of the Regency period. It stands in the grounds of a great mansion that has long been demolished, and Marius has refused to modernize it.

'There is no drama in a modern house,' he once said to me. 'When *you* want light, you press a silly switch. When *you* want a bath, you turn a silly tap. Whereas I have endless adventures stumbling about with candles and bending over water-butts. It is extremely good for the figure. And it is excellent training for the post-Atomic era, which I gather will shortly be upon us.'

Miss Mint had been Marius's governess, some thirty years ago, and when he introduced her to me he said:

'This is Miss Mint, who taught me everything that I know.'

'Not quite everything, Marius,' she answered, gently, with the quick flush that was always coming and going in her cheeks. 'A little botany, perhaps.'

'You taught me, at least, that flowers feel. And that, therefore, everything feels. That was a more important lesson than anything I ever read in the history books. Though of course, I might have learned it from Pythagoras.'

'Oh Marius, do you really remember Pythagoras?' she asked, eagerly.

'Of course I remember Pythagoras!' And then, noticing that I was mystified, he turned to me and said: 'I should explain that Miss Mint always related her lessons to me in terms of flowers. They even crept into the geometry. And so, when she was explaining the theory of Pythagoras, she told me the story of the bean-field, which is far more important than all the right-angled triangles in the universe.'

I confessed that I had never heard about Pythagoras and the bean-field.

'It is short and sweet. The bean-field killed him. Pythagoras, of course, was a vegetarian, and he had such a reverence for plants and flowers that he refused to cross the bean-field when he was escaping from his enemies. He would have trampled some of the beans to death. So he kept to the road, and was killed by the Agrigentines. You see how much you have missed by neglecting to engage Miss Mint as an instructor. However, as she is coming to live among us you may have an opportunity of making up for lost time.'

Miss Mint, at this point, was engaged in conversation by Our Rose, who bore down on her with the obvious intention of picking her brains. Marius led me into a corner to explain what he meant by Miss Mint coming to live among us.

It was a simple story. How was I to guess, as I listened to it, through the quiet murmur of feminine conversation, that it was to lead to such turgid drama, such Machiavellian intrigue?

Miss Mint, it seemed, had come into a small legacy. Three thousand pounds, which would go towards buying an annuity, and enable her to retire from the distasteful task of educating the small and spotty son of an opulent politician. And not only three thousand pounds, but two little Tudor cottages, one of which – Briar Cottage – lay on the other side of the woods about a quarter of a mile away. In this cottage she proposed to settle down and to end her days. But this would only be possible, with any degree of comfort, if she could sell the other cottage, which bore the unfortunate name of Bide-a-Wee.

The term Bide-a-Wee derived, not from Hawaii, as might be imagined, but from Perth, and had been bestowed upon it by Miss Mint's late aunt, in a fit of whimsicality. She had never lived there, having cherished the hope that she might some time come South and bide a wee herself. This ambition was never realized. However, during her lifetime the old lady had derived a great deal of vicarious pleasure from Bide-a-Wee, by making it even more Tudor than it was already, filling it with synthetic ingle-nooks, reproduction turnspits and bogus Welsh dressers, which she ordered from the catalogues of the great emporiums of Glasgow and Edinburgh. It was now frenziedly picturesque and agonizingly uncomfortable; it was, in short, a 'highly desirable' property, as property is assessed in these days.

'Miss Mint has charged me with the disposal of it,' said Marius. 'I shall try to find an extremely tall stockbroker who will slowly stun himself to death on the oak beams.'

'How much do you expect to get for it?'

'At least four thousand. It is far too vulgar to fetch a penny less. Miss Mint, at last, will have enough to be able to sit down for a little while, and think. She thinks, I may say, extremely well, as you will discover when you get to know her better.'

But alas . . . it was to be a long time before I was to know Miss Mint better. Only a few days after the party by candle-light, she was stricken with a violent attack of shingles. For some weeks her sight was despaired of, and she lay, a shrivelled little bundle of pain, staring through dark glasses at a world that was filled with even more menacing shadows than before. Summer was well advanced before she was on the road to recovery.

In the meantime, a great many things had happened.

And one of them was Erica Wyman.

§ I I I

Erica Wyman was famous. Ever since the publication of her best-selling gypsy novel *Where My Caravan Has Rested,* she has been an established celebrity, and she was firmly deter-mined to remain one. She was not at all embarrassed when her friends hinted that the caravan had usually rested in places less romantic than her prose would seem to suggest, such as the Metropole Hotel at Brighton. She laughed to scorn the slander that her principal source of Romany information was a middle-aged dentist who had once made a fortune by reading the predictions of Mr. Petulengro, and applying them to the turf. 'Jealousy, my dear: nothing but jealousy,' she would retort. And so assured was she, and so industrious, that whenever an editor wanted an article on gypsies – and editors seem to be in an almost constant state of wanting articles on gypsies – they would automatically apply to Erica Wyman.

She was, in short, the Gypsy Queen of the literary world, and as such she was not precisely my cup of tea. For, if the truth be told, I have never been greatly enamoured of gypsies. The few I have known were dirty and avaricious. There is only one man living who can write about gypsies without being a bore. He is Rupert Croft-Cooke. But then Rupert has lived and travelled with them, has learned to speak their language, and in any case is very much of a bohemian himself.

Apart from Rupert's gypsies, you can have the lot. It is a moot point whether they are more tedious on the stage of a theatre or in the pages of a novel. Maybe the theatre has it. In every gypsy operette there is always a *scène a faire* in which they bite each other's wrists, or do something equally repulsive, to an accompaniment of wailing arpeggios from the orchestra. After which the heroine, with her hands clamped permanently to her hips, like a sort of *ersatz* Carmen, skips away over the mountains with a great deal of mocking laughter, and an exit line which is almost certain to bring in something about 'the wind on the heath, brother'. One has had enough of that old tag of Borrow. As a motto for a bicycling club in Hackney it might serve very well, but constant reiteration has robbed it of its last echo of poetry.

'The wind on the heath, brother', was a phrase that was seldom far from the lips of Our Erica. She used it so often, and so automatically, that sometimes one suspected that she must have it embroidered on her underwear. She would whisper it sentimentally at cocktail parties, with her large lips protruding over the rim of a dry martini, lifting up her eyes, tossing her bobbed grey hair, and staring through the smoke, as though she were seeing a vision of the distant moors. When the occasion demanded she would vary it to 'a wind on the heath, sister' . . . with an artful little smile to show that the misquotation was deliberate. The line seldom failed to produce the effect she desired, namely, that she was at heart a simple gypsy, who longed to escape from all this metropolitan glamour and wander barefooted over the hills, and was only constrained from doing so by the demands of her genius, which chained her to her desk. In fact, she would have sharply resented any suggestion that she should continue to practise what she preached. The nearest she ever got to a caravan, after she became famous, was at the Ideal Homes Exhibition, when she was photographed sitting on the steps, stirring a large copper pot from which emerged fumes which smelled strongly of Chypre.

Such is the lady who now looms into view, walking down the lane by the side of Our Rose.

I had already heard of her arrival, through Miss Emily. She had telephoned to me that morning to ask me to play canasta on the following Tuesday. I said that I would be delighted, and asked if Our Rose would also be coming. 'Rose?' echoed Miss Emily. 'Oh, I don't think we could ask *her*. Far too grand, nowadays! Haven't you *heard*? She has Erica Wyman staying with her. Yes – *the* Erica Wyman. Gypsies. Operator, I'm in the middle of a call. Yes, gypsies. What did you say? Really, this line is intolerable, I shall write to the . . . oh, that's better. Don't you? Can't you? I'm *so* glad to hear you feel like that about her books too. Neither can I. Not a word. But I suppose she *sells*. And she does get her name in the papers. And you know what Rose *is* . . . can be so charming, but when it's a question of publicity . . . What? I said, you know what Rose *is* . . . operator, operator. . . .'

The conversation had trickled out in a sequence of kettle drums, horn blasts, minor sixths and all the other orchestral effects which, in these days, accompany telephone calls in the South of England. However, in spite of the interruptions, I had been able to gather how the land lay. Our Rose had acquired a celebrity, and Our Rose was evidently keeping the celebrity strictly to herself. In other words, battle was the order of the day. It was all very enjoyable and slightly insane. After all, it was midsummer. And if there is not a hint of madness in our midsummers, if there is not a tinge of lunacy in the burning skies and the drowsy shadows, then there is no sense in having midsummer at all.

But we must get back to the lane, with Erica and Rose advancing towards us.

'Good afternoon.'

'Good afternoon.'

There were the usual spasmodic sentences about how long it was since we had met, and what were we writing now . . . a question which always worries me because I can never think of anything to say but 'a book' – an answer which may be true but can hardly be described as a riposte. While these inanities were being trotted out, I took the opportunity of studying Miss Wyman at close quarters. Everything about her was sharp and dark. She had a sharp nose, sharp dark eyes, sharp shoulders, and a sharp mouth enhanced with a deep lipstick. Her voice was so sharp that you felt her vocal chords were over-strung. She wore a sharp, mannish, tailored suit of dark heather tweed, and her only concession to Bohemia was a dark red scarf which, believe it or not, was embroidered with a *motif* of black caravans. Even this was pinned with a sharp jet brooch in the shape of a crescent moon. In spite of this sharpness she was intensely and aggressively feminine.

'What brings you down to this part of the world?' I asked.

The question appeared to affect Miss Wyman with a sharp attack of coyness. She glanced at me, then she glanced at Our Rose, then she lowered her eyes, and then she began to trace patterns in the dust with her shoe. 'Well . . .' she said. And then looked back at Rose and giggled. 'Shall we tell him?'

'Do you think we *should?*' breathed Our Rose.

'He's bound to find out, sooner or later.'

'But supposing it fell through?'

Miss Wyman flinched, and clutched Our Rose's arm. 'Don't say it – don't say it! It *mustn't* fall through!'

This was the sort of conversation that maddens me. What might, or might not, fall through? And why all this archery about it?

'Has something gone wrong?' I inquired.

'Oh no! Not yet!'

Our Rose could contain herself no longer. 'And it won't go wrong; something *tells* me that it won't!' She turned to me. 'I *must* tell you. Erica is going to buy Bide-a-Wee!'

This was indeed news, and I rapidly switched the corners of my mouth in an upward direction in order to assume a delight that I was far from feeling. For though it was nice to know that Miss Mint had got an offer, the prospect of Erica as a near neighbour was not so good. I foresaw all sorts of tiresome complications; there would be caravans on the village green, and women with babies at the front door, trying to sell one clothes-pegs. Worst of all there would be more photographers, for Erica had a very keen sense of the value of publicity.

However, for the moment she was Our Rose's responsibility. Our Rose had found her, as it were, and Our Rose could keep her. In the meantime, one must not be selfish. The main thing was that Miss Mint should get a good price for Bide-a-Wee, which, till now, had attracted very few offers. I did some rapid thinking.

'How wonderful!' I said. 'You *are* lucky. I thought it had gone.'

'Gone?' Erica looked at me in dismay. 'How could it have gone?'

'When? Who?' demanded Our Rose.

· 'There was a woman from London the other day,' I lied. 'She was mad about it.'

'That might have been me.'

'I don't think so. She was a widow. She came in a Rolls.' The woman from London was becoming quite real to me.

'Oh dear!' The ladies exchanged glances. 'Do you know how much she offered?'

'I couldn't say. Miss Mint's asking five thousand, isn't she?'

'Five? Good heavens no! Four!'

'You don't mean to say she's only asking four? Well – that *is* a bargain!'

'You really think so?' Erica gave me a searching look. 'We were *going* to offer three thousand five hundred. . . .'

'That was your idea, darling,' retorted Our Rose with some sharpness. 'I was all for snapping it up at once.'

'Oh dear! Perhaps I'd better telephone the agents when we get home and say that if four thousand really *is* the lowest. . . .'

'I certainly think you had,' I said. 'And I should send a deposit by tonight's post. Then it's bound to be yours.'

The momentary gloom introduced by my mythical lady from London was quickly dissipated by the thought that Bide-a-Wee was, as it were, in the bag, and we set off at a brisk pace down the lane.

'Of course,' said Erica, 'I shall change the name. Bide-a-Wee – quite impossible.'

'You could pronounce it Beedahwi,' I suggested. 'Then people might think it had something to do with gypsies.'

A frosty smile greeted this sally.

'I still think my idea is best,' exclaimed Our Rose. 'You should call it "Where my Caravan has Rested". Don't you agree?'

I did not. It seemed to me far too long. People would be tempted to abbreviate it into 'Where my C has Rested'. Which would sound peculiar. I could see it in my mind's eye:

> Miss Erica Wyman,
> Where my C has Rested.

They might even put 'Where my C has R'd', which would sound worse still. However, I was fortunately saved from putting these thoughts into words by Erica proclaiming that it would look like advertising, and if there was one thing she hated it was that.

'At any rate,' continued Our Rose, 'I'm sure that the name should have a gypsy atmosphere, don't you think?'

Erica said that she supposed people would expect it of her.

'*Can't* you think of anything?' she asked me. 'Titles always seem to come so easily to you.'

My facility with titles, at this moment, was indeed alarming. There were a hundred I should have liked to suggest. One of them was The Stewpot. But that might have been regarded as unfeminine. So in desperation I said: 'Why don't you just call it "The Caravan" and have done with it?'

The effect on the ladies of this somewhat pedestrian observation was remarkable. They gasped, they clapped their hands, they very nearly skipped. 'The Caravan' it should be, and how lucky it was that we had met, and what a genius I was.

'Or do you think', demanded Erica, in a sudden access of inspiration, 'that it should just be "Caravan"?'

More gasps from Our Rose, more exclamations. 'Caravan' was even more wonderful than '*The* Caravan'. Didn't I think so? Yes, I said, I did.

For I was rather bored with the whole discussion, and if it had gone on much longer I should have suggested 'Charabanc'. But here we were at the end of the lane, and the ladies must turn left to get their bus, and I must turn right to get my tea.

§ I V

At home, Marius was waiting for me in the music-room, with 'Four' sitting on his knee.

'Something tells me,' he said, 'that you have heard the news.

'Yes, I met them in the lane. How did you learn to stroke "Four" like that?'

'Am I stroking him in any particular way?'

'You know you are. Very firmly on the neck and down the spine and up the tail, so that. . . .'

'So that I have a somewhat closer view of his posterior than seems immediately necessary.' Marius gently deposited 'Four' on the carpet and brushed a speck of fur from his trousers. 'She's a monster, isn't she?'

'Yes. But that's hardly the point, if she's prepared to pay.' I told him of my imaginary lady from London and Erica's intention of making an immediate offer.

Marius nodded, but he did not seem as pleased as I had hoped, Something seemed to be weighing on his mind.'

'Don't you think she *will* make the offer?'

'I have no doubt that she will. That's not the trouble. The trouble is Miss Mint.'

'What about her?'

'She is far too good. She is the only woman I have ever met who is quite incapable of telling a lie.'

'Why should she need to tell a lie?'

'She will have to tell a very big lie indeed if she ever hopes to sell her cottage. And if she doesn't tell it – or if somebody doesn't tell it for her – she will never sell the cottage at all.'

'But *why*?'

'Because of the water.'

'What's wrong with the water?'

'Nothing at all, as far as I know.' Marius took a long puff on his cigarette. 'It merely doesn't exist. The well has run dry.'

CHAPTER SIX

THE WELL

HERE, as they say, was a pretty kettle of fish. We were all, in one way or another, involved in the affairs of Miss Mint. She had come into our lives, and whether we liked it or not, she had come to stay. In fact we did like it, and we would not let her down. But in the meantime, it was vital that she should sell her cottage.

'Are you sure the well has run dry?'

'Quite sure. I was over there this afternoon. It's so dry that it isn't even damp.'

'Does she know?'

'Obviously not. If she had known, she would have told us. I doubt if anybody knows – even the agents, who are quite honest people. The cottage has been untenanted for a number of years, and when they last inspected it, the well was full.'

'It might rain, or something, and fill up again.'

'If one knows anything about wells,' observed Marius – and from his tone I was convinced that one knew quite a lot about wells, and that one could probably lecture on them at considerable length – 'one would suggest that this particular well will not fill up again until the middle of October. One might of course be wrong. It might be the beginning of October, if the season were exceptionally inclement. It certainly would not be before.'

'But supposing Erica sent her ten per cent deposit tonight, would she be able to get out of it, legally?'

'One can get out of anything, legally, until the contract is actually signed.'

'So Miss Mint has had it?'

'That depends.'

'On what?'

At that moment the telephone rang. I went to answer it. It was Erica, and might she speak to Marius if he was still with me?

Marius took the receiver. 'Good Evening! Ah yes, about the cottage. Really? I'm so glad. Yes, it is a charming little place, isn't it? I think you'd be very happy there. I beg your pardon? A final inspection? Yes, of course. I have the keys. Tomorrow? I'm afraid that would be impossible. Thursday? Would you mind holding the line a moment while I look at my book?'

He cupped his hand over the receiver.

'My dear Beverley' he said, 'have you any criminal tendencies?'

'Dozens.'

'Are you prepared to use them in a good cause?'

'Most certainly.'

'And are you disengaged for the next few days?'

'I am.'

'In that case, I will start the ball rolling.'

He spoke again into the telephone. 'Alas! I'm afraid the first time I can manage is Sunday afternoon. I beg your pardon? Oh no . . . I don't think there is any danger of *that*,

particularly if you send your deposit tonight. But of course. There are always those last-minute details, aren't there? You *can?* Splendid! Then . . .' a faint pause . . . 'then supposing we have a little cocktail party at six o'clock? Yes . . . at the cottage itself. And we will go over everything, and drink to your future happiness! At six o'clock then, on Sunday. Good night!'

He sat down heavily, and passed his hand over his forehead.

'I can never understand why so many criminals are obese. I lost pounds during that conversation.'

'What *is* all this?'

'I will explain. Would you, in certain circumstances, be prepared to play a little trick upon our friend Erica? To practise a certain amount of deceit?'

'I would play a very large and very dirty trick upon her,' I replied. 'And I would deceive her to the hilt with the utmost pleasure on every possible occasion.'

'Thank you. Now for the physical problem. Would you be prepared – let me see, today is Wednesday – would you be prepared to set aside the nights of tomorrow, Friday and Saturday for some rather violent physical exercise?'

'What sort of physical exercise?'

'Never mind what sort.'

'Not cricket?'

'Cricket is not physical exercise. Cricket is a state of mind.'

'Then what?'

'Building. And Fetching. And Carrying.'

There was a moment's pause, in which I stared at Marius in bewilderment.'

And then it came out, the whole enchanting plan, the conspirator's plot which was to save the fortunes of Miss Mint, and incidentally to give me three of the happiest evenings of my life.

§ 11

It could not have been simpler. The plan was to fill Miss Mint's well by buckets of water taken from the stream which trickled through the copse that bordered Our Rose's estate. In order to obtain enough water for this purpose, it would be necessary to build a dam in one of the secret hollows of the copse.

When I said that the plan 'could not have been simpler' I was exaggerating. It could, in fact, have been very much simpler. For one thing, the only place where we could build the dam was at least a hundred yards away from Miss Mint's well. And after a few hours, the transport of heavy buckets of water through fields of long grass, on a hot night in July, might prove to be a diversion that would pall.

For another, we would run a grave risk of being detected by Our Rose and Erica themselves. The stream, after leaving the copse, ran through Rose's garden. If it were suddenly to dry up she would become suspicious, and start prowling about upstream, and maybe surprise us in our nefarious activities. That stream meant a lot to Our Rose. On the back of the rustic garden seat which faced her lily-pond she had painted, in Gothic letters.

> Men may come, and men may go
> But I go on for ever.

Which was true in more senses than one.

What would these ladies do if, one night, while they were reclining on the poetical seat, there were to be an awful gurgle, and a sort of hiccup, and the water dried up in a waste of mud? They would obviously get up and do something, and it would almost certainly be unpleasant.

Finally, there was the gravest risk of all, that Miss Mint herself might discover what had happened. True, there was no chance of that at the moment, for she would not be able to

leave the hospital for at least another fortnight. But afterwards? When she returned, and was confronted by an enraged
Erica standing over an empty well, accusing her – as she un-
doubtedly would – of having sold the cottage under false
pretences? Even the faintest suspicion that she had been
guilty, however inadvertently, of straying from the strictest
paths of rectitude would be an appalling shock to her nervous
system.

However, it was no use crossing these bridges before we
came to them. The immediate problem was to fill the well
before Sunday.

Three of us were involved in the adventure, Marius, myself,
and my old friend Cyril who, though he is now a distinguished
critic, still carries with him the atmosphere of the ward-room.
Cyril spent the afternoon spying out the land, and returned
with the news that he had found the perfect spot for building
the dam. All seemed set fair.

It was nearly ten o'clock when Marius's car purred slowly
up the lane, curved into the little crescent, and stopped outside
the front door. As it did so, there was an alarming rattle of
buckets from inside.

'Good heavens!' exclaimed Gaskin. 'It's enough to wake
the dead.'

I had not realized that Gaskin was coming with us. As I
turned, I saw that he was dressed with exceptional elegance.
He looked as if he were about to sally forth into the Burlington
Arcade to buy quantities of very expensive toilet water.

'Gaskin . . .' I began, surveying his immaculate attire.

'Mr. Marius asked me to come and keep watch,' said Gaskin.
Then he added . . . 'Somebody's got to look respectable on this
expedition. Supposing you were to run into the police?'

I felt tempted to suggest that the sight of so *soignée* a
figure, sitting in a dark country lane at midnight, would
probably give the police peculiar ideas. Then I remembered
that Gaskin had always been on the most cordial terms with

half the constabulary of Surrey, so I held my peace. One might well be thankful for Gaskin's presence. One usually is.

Half an hour later we were creeping through the coppice, finding our way by the light of the moon, which cast a filigree of silver shadow through the branches. The night was breathlessly still; even the poplars were standing to attention; and we had to hold the buckets close to our sides to prevent them from rattling. Then we heard the trickle of the stream.

'This is the place,' said Cyril.

§ I I I

Nearly everything that I love in life seemed suddenly to be happening all at once.

Moonlight – summer – a silent wood – a secret stream – friends to share it. And now, the supreme pleasure of building a dam.

Dam-making, surely, must be one of the most exquisite pleasures which life can afford, even if the dam is only a scrabble of sand on the seashore, hastily thrown up to make a pool in the wake of the retreating tide. My love of dams is so unreasonable that the psychiatrists would surely find it morbid; they would say that the dam was a symbol of the womb, or something equally sickly, and the pool was a symbol of suppressed desire, which in a sense it is, as I cannot suppress my desire to fill it with shrimps – or, in the case of a fresh-water stream, with sticklebacks. (The shrimps and sticklebacks, of course, would be symbols of sadism.)

But this dam . . . even the most fervent psychiatrist could have found nothing nasty to say about it. For one thing, it smelt so delicious. It was made of small granite rocks, and clods of moist earth, and fallen twigs and stumps that had the roots of wild white violets still clinging to then. When you bent down and lifted a lump of soil, the scent of the broken herbs and mosses was like a benediction. Again, it sounded so enchanting. As the two sides came nearer together, the *legato* trickle of the water was gradually hastened; it turned to an *allegro*, and to an *allegretto* . . . and just before Marius dropped the final, central stone, into a shrill *presto*.

Then it began to fill. There were breathless scramblings up the bank to fetch more turf and more rocks to hold it, and a brilliant naval manœuvre, on the part of Cyril, to form a conduit to take the overflow. At last we could dip our buckets, and race away.

And then up the slope, through the undergrowth, over the hedge, and out into the open field, with the long grasses lacing our ankles and the full moon shining diamond-bright on the water in the buckets. By the time we reached the well in Miss Mint's tiny garden we were usually out of breath, and we would pause with our buckets on the edge of the brickwork before the big thrill of pouring in the water. Then, with a one, two, three, over they went, and six dancing flashes of silver shot into the darkness below. We could just see a ghost of white froth and hear the drip of water from the old walls.

'It is almost impossible to believe,' I said to Marius, 'that anything so agreeable as this can actually be in a good cause.'

'Let us hope you still feel so when the night is over,' he observed. 'In the past few minutes I have been making a slight calculation.' He glanced at a sheet of notepaper in his hand. 'Assuming that each of these buckets contains two and a quarter gallons, and that one eighth of a gallon is lost in transit, and assuming that the well has a depth of forty feet, a circumference of twelve feet, and a cubic capacity of . . .'

'The only cubic capacity that interests me at the moment,' interrupted Cyril, 'is my own cubic capacity for several pints of lager. Iced.'

'I was only trying to be helpful.'

'Bless you. I know you were. But what does it all mean in the end?'

Marius peered closer over his notes. 'It means', he said, with a note of triumph, 'that it will be necessary for us, in the course of the next three days, to cover a distance of approximately forty-five miles between us, bearing some fifteen hundred gallons, which, in terms of avoirdupois, is. . . .'

I cannot remember what it was in terms of avoirdupois. All I know is that by the time the last bucketful was poured in, at midnight on Saturday, it felt as though it must have been several tons.

We sat down by the side of the well, tired out but supremely happy, and gloated over the black circle of water which glimmered in the moonlight. Suddenly in the background there was a loud pop. It was Gaskin with the champagne, which I had ordered to celebrate the occasion. We drank Miss Mint's health, and then I poured a drop of wine on to the surface of the water, for luck. 'We shall be able to tell Erica that her well has special properties,' I said, 'and that she ought to bottle the water.'

'There are a great many things that Miss Wyman should bottle,' retorted Marius, with a yawn. 'And the first thing is herself.'

With which we went home to bed.

§ I V

But all was not yet plain sailing. There remained the question of the pump, or rather the question of turning the starting-handle of the engine which ran the pump. We had not realized that this would present any problem because we had been misled by a card which was hanging on the wall of the pump-shed. This was headed 'Service Directions for the Eureka Pump', and it began with a section 'To Start the Pump'. Accompanying it was a brightly coloured picture entitled 'A

Child Can Turn It!' To prove the truth of this statement the artist had portrayed a frail and exquisite female infant, dressed as for a party, languidly curling her tiny fingers round the starting-handle which, as a result of these attentions, was rotating in a whirl of arrows.

This picture, as we were now to discover, was a gross example of commercial wishful thinking. There may have been a time in the past when the pump would have responded to these infantile caresses, though I doubt it. But now, if an entire orphanage had been attached to the handle and whirled round by some exterior force, the pump would still have stuck. Even Cyril, who is as strong as an ox when he feels inclined, could not make it budge.

This disturbing discovery was not made till after five, and the ladies were due to arrive at six. It was one of the first times I had seen Marius really upset. 'It's precisely the sort of idiotic detail that would make a woman back out of the whole thing,' he declared.

'You can hardly call the water supply an idiotic detail.'

'If we can't make it work today, she may insist on trying tomorrow, and by then the water may have begun to sink again.'

'It's sinking already' observed Cyril. 'It's six inches below last night's level.'

'Can't *somebody* do something?'

We both looked at Cyril, who replied, tersely, that he had already acquired an outsize in blisters, a crick in the back and an incipient rupture, and that he was damned if he was going to do any more.

At precisely that moment a car drew up in the lane. For one horrifying moment we imagined that the ladies were already upon us. But no, it was our old friend Bob, who had taken advantage of the fine afternoon to motor down to Merry Hall, and had been sent on to the cottage by Gaskin.

As quickly as possible we explained the situation to him. I

had been afraid that he might be bored by the whole business; instead he was enchanted.

'*How* lucky that I arrived!' he exclaimed, with a positive tattoo of chain-rattling. 'George!'

'Yes, sir?'

'Go and see if the pump will work. And George. . . .'

'Yes, sir?'

'Don't strain yourself, because we've got a long drive home. And George. . . .'

'Yes, sir?'

'There's a very pretty variegated *ivy* on the pump-shed, and when you've started the pump you might pick some of it and put it in the *car*.'

George had no more luck with the pump than anybody else, and emerged, a few minutes later, looking very red in the face.

Bob did not seem at all disturbed. 'Never mind,' he said. 'Go and get the ivy. And Marius, don't look so depressed. We shall think of something.'

'I really can't imagine what.'

'The first thing, my dear, is to get them absolutely *plastered*. And then to show them round the house and be so charming to them that they'll think they're going to be *assaulted*, my dear. Have you any ice? Good. Then I shall make a cup. George!'

'Yes, sir?'

'Get the basket out of the car.'

The basket proved to be an elaborate cocktail cabinet, fitted into the back of the car, which Bob always carried about with him.

'If you give women a *cup*, my dear, they automatically assume that it is the sort of cup they make themselves, which is composed of a bottle of grocer's Graves, six syphons of soda water, and half a rancid cucumber. This will be a different sort of cup.' To prove his point he began it with half a bottle of Armagnac, and a tumblerful of Cointreau, observing that the ice could be put in at the last moment and that George must go out and look for some mint.

The next twenty minutes were spent in opening the French windows, moving a table out on to the terrace, and adding some of Marius's contributions to the already explosive cup. During this time there was a great deal of whispering and conspiring between Bob and George, and frequent return visits to the pump-shed, but Bob refused to divulge what was at the back of his mind. 'Wait and see, my dear,' was all he would say. 'Trust to your beady old friend.'

Punctually at six the ladies arrived – Our Rose very summery in flowered muslin, and Erica distinctly gypsophilian with a red bandana round her head, and long gold ear-rings. They were both pleasantly flattered by the presence of so many males, and obviously impressed by Bob, and the combination of his immense Daimler, his immaculate George, and above all, his golden chain with its glittering accompaniments, which he promptly produced from his pocket to light their cigarettes.

'*Too* charming,' murmured Erica. 'The keys, the charms, the lighters, the rings, the compasses.' She pointed to the champagne 'twizzler'. 'And what is that?'

'That, my dear, is a piece of sheer Semitic vulgarity,' he replied, with a disarming smile. 'And please call me Bob. Everybody does. And I shall call you Erica, which is really very nice of me, considering that I absolutely *loathe* the sight of you, my dear.'

Erica blinked, but before she could make any comment he continued: 'This divine cottage! Exactly what I was looking for, and you go and snap it up for only six thousand pounds. . . .'

'Four,' corrected Erica.

'Four?' Bob sank on to a bench, apparently prostrated. 'Four? I can't believe it. There must be some snag.'

'That's what we've come to see.'

'Well, let us start seeing at once.'

He rose to his feet. 'But first, Marius, may we have a teeny glass of your delicious cup?'

George began to hand it round.

'Such a good idea, cup, in this heat,' observed Our Rose. 'I'm sure a cocktail would have gone to my head.'

She took a considerable gulp of it, and blinked.

'I must make you one of my own cups one day,' said Erica. 'A secret gypsy remedy. Nearly all herbs. Practically no alcohol.'

'Then it must be very like this,' remarked Bob, handing her a large tumblerful. '*This* is mothers' milk.'

Erica gulped, and also blinked. 'Yes,' she said, 'it is. But mine has more . . . more . . . what shall I say?' Instead of saying it, however, she took another gulp.

'It's madly refreshing, don't you think?' demanded Our Rose, with an unaccountable giggle.

Erica nodded solemnly. 'Delicious. But surely there is a little . . . a little brandy?'

'Yes, there is, my dear. *What* a palate you have!'

'One has to have, in these days,' she replied, obscurely. And she too gave an unaccountable giggle.

It was thus in a somewhat roseate mood that the ladies began the tour of the house, and since Bob was constantly by their side, replenishing their glasses, it is hardly surprising that Our Rose, with a great deal of girlish laughter, declared that if she bumped her head on the beams again she would begin to feel quite dizzy. And it was only to be expected that Erica, by the time that we had finished with the house, and were going round the garden, had ceased to use the word 'gypsy', which was beginning to sound excessively sibilant, like 'gypshjee', and had substituted the more easily articulated 'Romany'.

Meanwhile, Marius was here there and everywhere, always

with the right word, the right suggestion . . . and when any danger arose, the right story, so that by the time the ladies had listened to it, we had moved on, and the danger was forgotten.

Thus, when we paused by a bed of violets, and Erica detected a slight crack in the wall above them, Marius pointed to the violets and said:

'I trust that you have a good cook?'

Erica stared at him blankly.

'I can never see a bed of violets without thinking of Walter Savage Landor,' continued Marius, taking Erica gently by the arm – a support which she was beginning to need – and steering her past the crack. 'One day, Landor threw his cook out of the window. As soon as he had done so he was smitten with remorse. He rushed downstairs, and into the garden, where she was lying with a broken leg. And he ran his hands through his hair and he cried, "Good God! I had forgotten the violets!" '

'It's working like magic, my dear,' whispered Bob. 'And now, get them all to sit down, and begin to talk about the well, and leave the rest to me.'

When we returned to the terrace Erica sat down on the bench with a bump, declined a further instalment of cup, and stated – very firmly – that she would like a glass of cold water. That gave me my chance.

'I think you should have it from your own well,' I said.

'There!' exclaimed Rose, raising herself abruptly from the somewhat somnolent position into which she had fallen. 'I knew there was something we'd forgotten. The well. We must look at it.'

'Yes,' agreed Erica, with a faint hiccup. 'Must look at well.' But she showed no immediate inclination to do so.

'It may have dried up,' continued Rose, shaking her head in a maudlin manner. 'They often do.'

Erica nodded. 'Heaps of times. I remember I once knew a gypshjee . . .' She did not finish the sentence.

Bob sprang to his feet. 'I'm mad about wells. I shall go and see.' He disappeared round the corner of the house, to return a moment later. 'Full to the brim, my dear. And the most delicious sparkling water you ever tasted.'

'But how do we get it out?' demanded Erica. She was beginning to look obstinate and obstreperous, as well she might, considering all that she had consumed.

Marius told her about the pump.

'Does it work?'

Before he could answer, Bob had leapt to his feet, explaining that he was mad about pumps, too, and that he would go and start it himself. Once more he disappeared round the corner of the house, closely followed by George, who had been lurking in the bushes.

What was going to happen now, I could not imagine. We sat there waiting, glancing furtively at one another, in an uneasy silence which was occasionally broken by brief and gloomy remarks from Erica about the general uselessness of pumps. She was obviously feeling more and more liverish.

Still we waited. Still nothing happened.

'I told you so,' proclaimed Erica. 'It doesn't work.'

At that moment Bob hurried back, wiping his hands on a silk handkerchief. Before the ladies could turn their heads he had given us a stage wink.

'My dear,' he cried. 'The most terrible thing. I've dropped my *chain*, my dear.'

'Not into the well?' exclaimed Erica, sitting up sharply.

'No. Into the engine. And if we start it going, it'll be ground to pieces!'

'Oh really!' Our Rose sank back on the rustic bench. 'What a misfortune! That beautiful chain!'

'But perhaps if we started the engine,' proposed Erica, somewhat callously, 'it might shake itself out in a few minutes?'

'It might, my dear,' retorted Bob, 'and it might not. It might also wreck the engine in a few seconds.'

'Oh! So it might. I hadn't thought of that.'

'Evidently not, my dear.'

'But I want to see the engine *going*,' insisted Erica.

'Well, in that case we shall have to wait and see what George can do.' Bob put his hand in his pocket with the evident intention of rattling, and tapped his foot impatiently when he found nothing there.

At this point George emerged from behind the bushes.

'Any luck, George?'

'No sir. It's way down inside, tangled up in the fly wheel.'

'I suppose we couldn't cut it?' suggested Erica.

Bob gave her a very beady look. 'My dear,' he said, 'I hate to seem difficult, but there happen to be nine sorts of gold woven into that chain. Nine, my dear.'

'Nine,' echoed Our Rose, reprovingly, to Erica.

'I heard you the first time,' retorted Erica.

'It would be a *sin* to cut it,' insisted Rose.

'Then how are we to know whether the pump works at all?'

'Just a moment.' It was Bob again. He swallowed a very large gulp of cup to fortify him in the climax of his act. 'Do you know what sort of make this pump is?'

'How should I?'

'Eureka! That's what it is. Eureka!'

'What has that got to do with it?'

'George!'

'Yes, sir?'

'What was the name of that wonderful pump we had at my cottage?'

'Eureka, sir' replied George, not batting an eyelid.

Bob nodded triumphantly. 'You see? What did I tell you?'

Erica was still looking suspicious. 'But was it easy to work?'

'Easy? My dear, a *child* could work it. George!'

'Yes, sir?'

'Do you remember that *ghastly* child who got into the pump-shed? The one with the rash?'

'Yes, sir.'

'Tell Miss Wyman what happened.'

The baffled expression on George's face warned Bob that his servant might be nearing the end of his capacities.

'No. I'll tell her myself.' He turned to Erica. 'My dear,' he said, 'there was this terrible child. Absolutely *covered*, my dear, and she might have given it to the dogs. One never knows. Does one?'

Erica, equally baffled, agreed that one didn't.

'How she got in,' continued Bob, 'no one will *ever* know. But when one has *seven* gardeners, my dear, all eating their heads off and not pulling up a *weed*, what can one expect? Anyway, there she was. Wasn't she, George?'

'Yes, sir.'

Our Rose suddenly came to life, with a hiccup.

'Where was she?'

'In the pump-shed, my dear.'

'And what did she do?'

'She started the pump.'

'Why?'

'My dear, you do ask the strangest questions. All I'm trying to tell you is that there was this *hideous* child, who could hardly *walk* . . . could she, George?'

'No, sir.'

'Who got into the pump-shed and just started it with a flick of the wrist.'

'How do you know she started it with a flick of the wrist?' demanded Erica.

'Well, my dear, she could have started it with a flick of anything you like. I should have *thought* it would have been the wrist.'

'But what does all this add up to?'

Bob rose impatiently to his feet. 'My dear,' he said, 'I give you up. If a tiny child – she was practically a *midget* – can go into a pump-shed, *covered* with the most repulsive rash – and start a pump that floods practically the whole of Kent, I should have thought that *you* might have been able to summon up enough energy to turn a handle and get a *teeny* bath, my dear.'

How Erica would have reacted to this onslaught will never be known. She was certainly growing very red in the face. But suddenly Bob stiffened, like a pointer on the scent, and gazed fixedly at the base of an old damson tree.

'George,' he murmured. 'Chives!'

'Yes, sir.'

'Did you bring the trowel?'

'Yes, sir.'

'Then go and fetch it from the car.' Bob turned to Erica. 'You don't mind, my dear? The only way I can ever keep a cook is to *smother* her with chives. And you seem to have acres of them. Not that they're precisely yours . . . yet. Though if you want the advice of a beady old member of The Race, my dear . . . which, judging from your expression, you don't . . . you'll see that they're yours tomorrow, and sign the contract. Goodbye. Goodbye Marius, and thank you for your delicious cup. And perhaps Beverley will come to the car and decide what must be done about my ridiculous chain.'

He wandered off, and I followed him. When we reached the car he said: 'I really did drop it, on purpose of course, and it was like a mother parting from her *child*, my dear. And I suppose we must lock up the pump-shed and leave it there till tomorrow when somebody comes to dismantle the engine. And here is George with the chives, and I must say I think he might have got a few more, considering the masses she has. However, I must be going. And listen! If that old *bag* doesn't buy the cottage, I promise faithfully to buy it myself.'

But she did buy it. On the following morning, at an early hour, she was at the estate agents, signing everything that came her way. A very nervous lady, the chief clerk thought, who complained bitterly of headaches, and constantly demanded large glasses of cold water.

CHAPTER SEVEN

P.G.

DIVINE Providence must have been watching over Miss Mint and her well, for as soon as Erica had set her signature to the contract, the floodgates of heaven were opened. It poured for the rest of July, it deluged throughout August, and the first week of September opened with a cataract. Crops were ruined, lawns were swamped, roses were battered into the mud. But Miss Mint's well – or rather, Erica's well, as we must now call it – remained full to the brim. Whereby we were spared a number of crises, legal, moral and domestic.

However, even if there had been a drought, and the well had dried up, it is doubtful whether Erica could have done much about it. By now, she had forfeited all claims to the affection of our little community. She had outraged Miss Emily by pouring scorn on her conduct at the canasta table; she had driven poor Miss Mint to tears by inserting a number of insulting clauses in the documents for the sale of the cottage; and she had profoundly shocked Mrs. Pattern, the vicar's wife, by informing her that *she* had no need of church, that *she* got her sermons from stones, and that *she* learned all she needed about God from the 'wind on the heath'. (Brother.)

'Whatever did you say to that?' I inquired.

Mrs. Pattern tossed her head. 'I said that it must be very inconvenient for her, as the nearest heath was sixty miles away. And that as she had no car she would have to go by train. And change at Dorking.'

Which was certainly one up to Mrs. Pattern.

The only person who maintained a pretence of friendship with Erica was Our Rose – for obvious reasons; Erica was still her guest at 'The Weathercocke', and until the alterations to Miss Mint's cottage were completed, she was likely to remain so. As Our Rose never cared to admit that her judgment might have been at fault, she pretended that everything in the garden was quite delicious. She continued to smile, but the smile was beginning to wear very thin.

How thin, I did not realize, till one day chance took me to 'The Weathercocke' when Rose was out. The Czechoslovakian maid admitted me and requested me to wait in the parlour. After a few minutes I was bored, and looked around for something to read. There was nothing but an old copy of *Vogue*, which I picked up, expecting to find in it some photographs of Rose's floral creations. I found something far more exciting. Out of it fell a quantity of postcards, bearing messages in Rose's handwriting, with many scarlet underlinings. The most cursory glance at these messages showed that they told a tale of acute domestic crisis. Thus:

> *There is no reason, known to US, for removing the nozzle of the hose. If, however, some person, either from perversity, or in order to satisfy some curious natural URGE, should feel impelled to remove it, would he or SHE be so obliging as to replace it?*

I blinked, and turned to the next.

> *The flowers in this house are, we HOPE, adequately arranged. However, should they not meet with the approval of SOME, we should be much obliged if the*

STALKS could at least be left standing in water, and not. . . .

Here there were several sentences which had been hastily scribbled out. Through the erasures I could read phrases like 'on the carpet', 'dripping on the veneer', and at the end, a mysterious note . . . 'special vase for HER? No. Where did she put pinholders?'

Curiouser and curiouser. Had these passionate proclamations, I wondered, been actually displayed? Or were they being held in reserve to mark the opening of hostilities?

I read on.

If it is NECESSARY to use this Frigidaire in the small hours of the morning, it would be most courteous if any persons so using it would not SLAM the door of it. Apart from the damage to the hinges, and the fact that such violence might dislodge the EGGS, such conduct is liable to awaken the entire HOUSEHOLD.

After this were more scribblings, and more mysterious phrases, such as 'GYPSY HABITS? Remind her still rationing in this country? Evidently forgotten. "Once a gypsy, always a gypsy"? No. "Never WAS a gypsy"? Libellous? "My mother said, that I never *should*", etc. Ask B. N.'

Just as I caught sight of my initials, I heard Rose's footsteps in the hall, and I only just had time to put back the postcards and replace the magazine before she opened the door.

There was now a sharp anti-climax. When I asked after Erica I was told that *dear* Erica was very well, and was in London for the day. How long was she remaining at 'The Weathercocke'? Oh – for several weeks more, she hoped. The cottage would seem quite different without dear Erica. I racked my brains for some means of bringing hoses and Frigidaires into the conversation, to say nothing of 'gypsy habits', but Rose steered skilfully away from these dangerous topics, and when I left I was no wiser than before. I would have to wait and see.

§ 11

I did not have to wait for long. Barely a fortnight later the crisis came to a head, on a stormy evening in October. I had just come in from the garden with a Bacchanalian basket of Autumn leaves . . . sprays of spindle with magenta berries, scarlet maples, bunches of paeony foliage which the early frosts had lit with a feverish glow, thorny twigs of hips and haws, and long trails of Virginia creeper that were scarlet at the tip, and gradually faded back through shades of rose and pink and amber. This exciting assortment was destined for a little black Nubian whom I had purchased a few days before. He stood on a Victorian pedestal in the music-room; his livery was brightly painted, and one arm held aloft a golden platter. He was delightfully vulgar and overdressed, and I hardly dared to think how delectable he would look, with all those reds cascading down over his peacock jacket and the dim light of the grille behind.

I heard footsteps and turned round. In the fading light, outside the conservatory, stood two familiar figures, Miss Emily and Our Rose. Really, this was too much. Why couldn't they use the front door and ring the bell in the ordinary way? Then I remembered that Gaskin was out. So I had to put down the berries and go and let them in.

They did hope, they said, as they wiped their shoes on the mat, that they were not disturbing me, and no, I must not dream of making any fresh tea, as they had already had it. And oh, what a lovely bunch of berries. Though it was a pity, added Rose, that all the leaves of the Virginia creeper would have fallen off by tomorrow morning, and that the spindle berries would probably have been trampled into my beautiful blue felt.

After these words of encouragement the two ladies seated themselves on opposite sides of the fire, and proceeded to fan themselves, as though they were suffering from some physical or mental fever, or possibly both.

As I had a suspicion that their business concerned Erica, it seemed best to take the bull – or perhaps one should say the cow – by the horns.

'And how are things at the cottage?' I asked Rose. 'Everything going splendidly?'

'How curious you should ask that!' said Rose. And then, to Emily: 'I think he must be psychic, dear.'

'It was about the situation at poor Rose's cottage that we really came to talk to you,' said Emily.

'But *is* there a situation? I thought that Erica. . . .'

'Erica!' Rose gave what is known as a hollow laugh. 'Erica! Don't speak to me about that woman!' She threw out her left arm and thrust an imaginary Erica into the fireplace. There was a moment's pause. Then she leant forward and fixed me with her moonstone eyes. 'Please correct me if I am wrong,' she said, 'but I don't believe that I can be called a *mean* woman.'

'Far from it.'

'Thank you. I do *not* give people copies of my books and then send them the bill. I do *not* buy specially small sherry glasses to save giving my friends a proper drink. Nor do I buy South African sherry, nor . . .' with a sort of snort . . . 'do I put water in it.'

As I had never heard of anybody else indulging in these singular activities, I assumed that they had some direct connection with Erica. I was right.

'*She* may care to do things like that,' continued Rose, with mounting tensity, 'but that is *her* affair. For all I know she may have her sherry glasses specially *designed*, to give a sort of optical illusion. I wouldn't be at all surprised.'

'Nor would I,' observed Miss Emily from her corner. 'In

fact, I could tell you something *else* that she does.' ' She opened her mouth very wide, as a prelude to her revelation, when Rose interrupted her.

'Thank you, dear,' she said, with some acidity. '*You* tell the story.'

'But no, darling,' protested Miss Emily. 'I was only going to say . . .'

'Yes, dear. Do say it. So much better.' And she leaned back, and regarded the ceiling, and hummed a faint tune to herself, as though she had lost all interest in the conversation.

'Please, Rose,' pleaded Miss Emily. 'After all, it *is* your story.'

'Is it?' She gave a brave little smile. 'Very well. If you insist.' She fixed me once more with the moonstone eyes.

§ I I I

'I believe you know that Erica is what is known as a paying guest?'

'Yes.'

'It is a quite simple arrangement. She has her own bedroom and her own sitting-room and all her meals, for . . . for so much a week.'

'How much *does* she pay?' I should not have asked the question, but I longed to know.

Rose sat up abruptly. 'Really! That is hardly the point!'

I should have thought that it was very much the point. But it was wiser to agree.

'The point, surely,' she continued, 'is that an agreement was made. And that having been made, it should be honoured.'

'Of course . . . of course.'

'Very well.' The moonstone eyes were beginning to look more like agates. 'As I said, the arrangement was that she should have all her meals. And she has had them. I am not complaining about that. Not in the least. Perhaps if I had known beforehand that she had come to my house with the set purpose of digging her grave with her teeth, I might have thought twice about it. Not for my sake, but for hers. It makes me sad to see anybody quite deliberately eating herself to death. Haven't I often said so, Emily dear?'

'You have indeed.'

'She never stops eating.'

'Never!' agreed Emily. 'Her mouth is never empty. Never!'

'Early morning tea,' continued Rose. 'With biscuits. *Petit beurre*. So difficult to get, nowadays. An *enormous* breakfast. Eggs every day. And you know that the only way to get eggs is if you know somebody on the bl . . .' She pulled herself up very quickly. Our Rose has very strong views about the black market, in public. 'Somebody on a farm,' she continued, without blinking an eyelid. 'Then coffee at eleven, with more *petit beurre*. An enormous lunch. An enormous tea. An enormous dinner. And even *then* she hasn't finished. She prowls about, looking for things to put in her mouth. It's like living with a raging hyena. The way she bangs the door of the Frigidaire alone. . . .'

'She doesn't go to the Frigidaire?' demanded Miss Emily.

'*Go* to it?' retorted Our Rose. 'She practically assaults it. I wonder it has any hinges left. In fact, it was because of the Frigidaire that we first had a little argument.'

'No! What happened?'

'I merely mentioned to her one morning that the kitchen was immediately below my bedroom, and that if the door of the Frigidaire was constantly banged throughout the night, I found it difficult to sleep.'

'What did she say?'

'She suggested that I should get a new Frigidaire. But I had an answer to *that* little piece of insolence. I told her that if she ate such quantities of frozen food in the small hours of the morning she would develop an ulcer.'

'One would have thought that she was a mass of ulcers already,' observed Emily.

'No doubt she is, dear,' said Rose. 'But may I just finish the story? Thank you. Well, this has been going on ever since she arrived, without a single break – till last Saturday afternoon. Not *one* meal has she missed, in twelve weeks. Whenever she has gone up to London for the day she has always waited till after luncheon, and got back for dinner, somehow or other, even if it nearly killed her. It may be ten or eleven or nearly midnight . . . she gets back. I believe that if she were asked to dine with the Lord Mayor and *bathe* in turtle soup, she'd refuse and get back to my house, because she'd feel that otherwise she might not be getting her money's worth.'

'Till last Saturday afternoon,' prompted Emily.

'What happened last Saturday afternoon?' I demanded.

'She went away for the night, and did not return till after tea on Sunday.'

'And then?'

'It was this morning that it happened. Every Monday morning she goes into Dora's little office – Dora is my secretary, you know – and gives her a cheque for the previous week. Well, when she went in to see her this morning . . .' and now Rose's voice deepened, and her words came more slowly and deliberately . . . 'when she went in to see her this morning, she said that *as* she had been away from after luncheon on Saturday to after tea on Sunday, and that *as* she had therefore missed three meals . . .' She shuddered and put her hands over her eyes. 'I can't go on.'

'But you *must* go on,' I cried. 'You can't stop there.'

Rose shook her head. 'It's too petty,' she protested. 'Too squalid. It makes me feel . . . ' She shook herself, as though an earwig had fallen down her neck. '*You* tell him, dear Emily.'

Dear Emily was only too eager to do so. 'She went in to Dora,' she began.

'Yes dear,' interrupted Our Rose. 'I've already told him that.'

'She went in to Dora,' repeated Miss Emily, in somewhat sharper tones, 'and said that as she had missed three meals she would naturally expect a reduction on the weekly bill!'

'No?'

'But yes,' nodded Rose, with a weary smile.

'I can't believe it!'

Rose shrugged her shoulders. 'It happens to be true.' She achieved a wistful laugh, and rose to her feet. 'Amusing, isn't it? But don't let's think any more about such tiresome things.' She moved towards my bunch of leaves and berries. 'How beautiful these are! Such a pity about the Virginia creeper.'

And with that I had to be content. Rose would drop no hint of the counter-measures which, I was convinced, she was already elaborating. Nor would Miss Emily. All that lady would vouchsafe was a dark hint that Erica would 'regret it' ... and that she would bitterly repent her meanness 'when the time came'. But when that time would be, and what form the repentance would be made to take, lay hidden in the mists of the future.

Meanwhile, other adventures were in store, of a pleasanter and more permanent nature.

CHAPTER EIGHT

CHAIRS AND TABLES

AUTUMN sped swiftly by. The lawn was a scurry of
drifting leaves; the last of the water-lilies rusted, and
the fish glided ever more slowly through the freshening
water. At night there was a nip in the air, and in the morning
the brave banks of Michaelmas daisies were silvered with the
early frost.

My mother used to say that autumn was her favourite time
of the year; often I think it is mine as well. The colours of
autumn are even more exciting than those of spring; they are
fickle and unpredictable; you never know what is going to
happen from one moment to the next. A sharp frost overnight,
and in the morning a thousand little bonfires will be flickering
in all the trees. There will be tongues of scarlet flame in the
maples, and of yellow flame in the elms; there will be dark
fires, deep in the guelder roses, so that when the wind blows
you see a sombre glow of leafy embers. The sumachs will be
smouldering, the thorns will be ablaze, and in the hedge at
the end of the coppice there will be many fiery miracles

among the brambles . . . leaf after glowing leaf, streaked and striped with orange and crimson and vermilion. And over them all, high up among the paling sycamores, there will be cloudy clusters of the wild clematis – Old Man's Beard – the billowing smoke of Nature's annual conflagration.

The scents of autumn are more exciting too; bitter-sweet and nostalgic and elusive. The mosses under the copper beech have a fragrance more haunting than any April blossom; and the last few roses of summer, which are almost scentless when you pick them out-of-doors, to save them from the frost, will fill a whole room with perfume when you bring them into the warmth of the house.

And now we must go into the warmth of the house ourselves, though I am almost ashamed of asking you to do so.

For Merry Hall is still almost empty. Yes, even in this third year, we are still sitting on cane chairs, still frenziedly shifting the Empire settee from the drawing-room to the music-room when anybody calls, still 'making do'. True, we have the blue chandelier, and the window with the old iron grille. And the bedside table is still revolving merrily, shooting out books in all directions – including some new ones of my own make. But the general atmosphere is distinctly barren.

'As though the bailiffs were *permanently* in residence, my dear,' as Bob used to say to me.

Gaskin took a very dim view of this situation, and was constantly urging me to spend less on the garden so that the house could have a chance.

'If you spent on the house a tenth of what you spend on the garden the place would be finished by now. Look at all those trees!' He pointed out of the window to a small forest that had been delivered by lorry that morning, and was now stacked in the drive, with the roots covered with straw. 'All last week you had three extra men planting and staking! And now another lot! And the driver said there was more to come! What they must have cost I do *not* like to think!'

'Well Gaskin, with the trees it's a question of *time*. If I were to wait till next winter I should lose a year's growth.'

'And then there was the greenhouse; eighty pounds that was.'

'But it had to be reglazed.'

'And the new greenhouse stove, nearly a hundred.'

'But the old one hardly kept the frost out.'

'It's that old man,' said Gaskin, referring to Oldfield. 'That's what it is. He only has to hint that he wants a thing and you give it to him. Whereas when it comes to the house . . . why, my kitchen lino's so worn out that one day I shall trip up on it and break my neck.'

This was so gloomy a prospect that I told Gaskin that he should have his new linoleum tomorrow. He was somewhat mollified. But not for long. Things came to a head one day when he greeted me with the news that a magazine had rung up to ask if they could come down on the following week to take photographs of the house.

'I told them that I did not think it would be convenient, sir,' he said.

'But Gaskin, why? It's good publicity.'

'Not when it's in *this* state. Look at this room. It's almost empty.'

We were standing in the drawing-room. It was a bitterly cold morning in November, and the room looked not only empty but bleak. True, it was charmingly proportioned; the windows had been squared and painted; and the white paper with its pale grey stripe was as elegant as could be. But there was no carpet on the floor, no pictures on the walls, and apart from the aforesaid Empire settee nothing but a few shabby chairs and a rickety table.

I walked over to the settee. 'We might get some chrysanthemums,' I suggested, without much conviction. 'And I could be taken sitting on this.'

'You've been taken sitting on it already,' Gaskin reminded

me. '*And* lying on it. *And* sitting on the edge. *And* standing behind it. People will think it's the only piece of furniture we've got.'

'It almost is.'

'Then it comes to what I said before. You'll have to buy some things. Or shut this room up altogether.'

'That would be just weakness.' Silence, broken by teeth-chattering. 'Supposing we took some of the garden furniture from the music-room and had it painted?'

'It would still look like garden furniture.'

'Not if we had velvet things made to put on the seats.'

'By the time you'd finished doing all that you'd have spent more than if you'd bought new chairs.'

'Well, there's the other divan. We could cover that.'

'Which other divan?'

'The old one with the wobbly legs.'

Gaskin pursed his lips. 'You gave me that for my room,' he said coldly.

'So I did.'

'I have to sit down *somewhere*,' he observed. A long-suffering sigh. '*Sometimes*.'

'I know. I'm sorry.'

'The wooden chair which I *had* been using,' continued Gaskin, 'has been taken to the music-room instead of the piano-stool.'

'The piano-stool! Well, what about that? At any rate, that would be a beginning.'

Gaskin raised his eyebrows. 'Considering the state it was in, I gave it to the man who brings the coke.'

'What did he say?'

'He didn't say anything. He just gave me a look.'

This was terrible. I was beginning to realize the somewhat elemental fact that if you have a large house, if you have no furniture, and if nobody shows any signs of giving you any, you have to go to a shop and buy it. And that furniture costs money. And that if you have already spent all your money, you cannot buy furniture. It needs no Einstein to follow this chain of reasoning, but somehow it had escaped me.

'There must be *something*,' I said in desperation. 'Is the attic absolutely empty?'

'There's nothing in it but the chafing-dish, and you couldn't sit on that.'

Gaskin, I thought, was becoming almost unnecessarily tart. It was on the tip of my tongue to tell him so, but at that moment he excused himself. A large van had drawn up in the lane outside.

I went to the window to look out. Two men were undoing the back of the van, and Gaskin was standing by their side. Then ... it happened. Through the door, with the men holding it very gingerly by the legs, came a chair, or rather, a masterpiece in carved walnut. Even on its side, with the hands of the men around it, its elegance and its perfection were eloquent.

Gaskin ran in, flushed with excitement. From Wych Cross, he said. Four of them. I nodded. I might have known it.

Wych Cross! It was a magic name to me. Wych Cross! And as I stood there on that grey morning, with the wind blowing through the open door, and the men tramping in with their precious burdens, I seemed to see again, as though it were a flash-back in a film, the strange genius who had created it.

§ 11

His name was Geoffrey Hart.

Geoffrey Hart was one of the few men I have ever known who was granted the title of genius not only by his friends but by his enemies, of whom he had plenty. His beginnings were conventional; he was head boy at Harrow and senior classical scholar at Trinity, and both of those distinctions he achieved,

as it were, *en passant*, for even as a schoolboy he was dreaming
of power. It was when he was still at Trinity that I met him.
I was a few years his junior and was somewhat over-awed by
him, even though he was still, in appearance, a pink and white
schoolboy. His rooms were so luxurious, his clothes so elegant,
the luncheon he gave me so exquisitely chosen, his conversation so *mondaine* . . . never, I thought, if I lived to be a
hundred, could I attain such poise or such polish.

Over a yellow Chartreuse – my first – he asked me my plans
for the future.

I told him that I was going to Oxford. After that, if I
could get a job, to Fleet Street. 'And you, Geoffrey, what are
you going to do?'

He puffed at a cigar, which looked strangely out of place
between his cherubic lips. He answered:

'I am going to make a million pounds.'

'Oh!' said I, for lack of any other comment. And then –
realizing that he was not expressing an ambition but making a
statement of fact: 'When are you going to make it?'

'With luck, by the time I am twenty-five. Without luck,
by the time I am twenty-seven.' Whereupon, he dismissed
the subject, as though it were not worthy of further discussion,
and informed me that it was time for him to go and see his
tutor.

Geoffrey made his million. Whether at twenty-five or
twenty-seven I could not say; it was certainly before he was
thirty. He made it by a series of swift and spectacular
manoeuvres in the City, largely in the gold market. He seemed
to have a sixth sense about gold. I remember talking about
him to a hard-bitten mining engineer who had spent his whole
life in the Rand. He had been discussing with Geoffrey a
complicated network of reefs – or veins or lodes or whatever
the technical word may be – and had been astonished by his
intricate knowledge of every detail of the structure. He gave
the impression that he could find his way about that mine in

the dark. 'But when did you last visit it?' asked my friend. Geoffrey smiled. He had never visited it – never even been to South Africa. He just knew.

Yes, this really is leading us to the walnut chairs, however indirectly. For all the time that Geoffrey was making fortunes, and losing them, he was building up one of the most remarkable collections of pictures and furniture in Europe. In this task he was aided – sometimes more than he realized – by the beautiful girl he had married, the only woman who ever held his heart. Her name was Dorothy. Today, her beauty is unimpaired, her intelligence at its most acute . . . and to be married to Geoffrey needed some intelligence! But she is alone. Geoffrey died at the end of the war, like a flame that is spent. No body could contain a spirit so eternally afire; he was physically burnt out, though even on his death-bed he still looked like the undergraduate who, in the years gone by, had told me that it was time to go and see his tutor. 'It's a bore to have to go and see one's tutor,' he had said then, 'but if one must . . .' He used almost the same phrase in the last words he ever spoke to me. 'It's a bore to have to go and see one's Maker' he said, 'but if one must. . . .'

So Dorothy was left alone, with the long galleries of masterpieces in the great house at Wych Cross. Van Dyck and Rembrandt greeted her in the hall, Rubens beckoned her from the staircase, she dined with Brueghel, she sat by the fire with Patinir, she went to bed at night past rows of Van Goyens. To keep these masters company was a collection of furniture such as few museums in the world can boast – the cream of the art of Chippendale, Queen Anne tables in gold and silver gesso, painted cabinets of fantastic workmanship, mirrors reflecting the gleam of priceless jade.

Among these pieces was a set of four chairs.

My chairs, which Dorothy had now given to me, in memory of one of the most remarkable spirits of his age.

§ III

If one were to say that one's life had been radically changed
by a set of walnut chairs, the statement might seem precious.
It is the sort of thing that aesthetes used to say in the 'nineties.
That does not worry me much. There were many periods in
history which were less worthy, in almost every respect, than
the eighteen-nineties, and one of them, in my humble
opinion, is the nineteen-fifties.

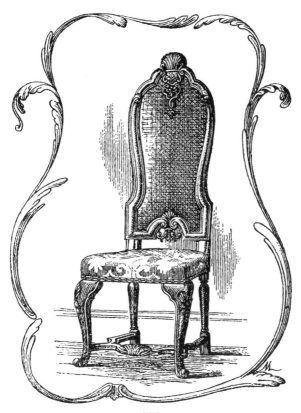

Anyway, my life was changed by these chairs; it was changed in the sense that it was both widened and balanced, and given a surer sense of direction. As we are now going to talk about those chairs at some length, I am asking our artist, Mr. McLaren, to draw a picture of one of them. Firstly, the whole chair:

Secondly, the detail of the decoration of the back.

I should explain that the walnut is the colour of old amber and dark honey, and that the velvet on the seats is a faded Rembrandt brown.

After the chairs had arrived, on that bitter morning, and after we had hurried out and lit a fire for them – (I had an idea that things so precious might catch a chill) – and after we had prowled round them and gloated over them, and looked at them from the back and the front, and even sat on them – (with bated breath) – I sent Gaskin out, shut the door, and made a vow.

The vow was that somehow or other, cost what it may, I would try to live up to those chairs. Again, that sounds like the 'nineties, and again I am unrepentant. To try to 'live up to' anything beautiful, whether it is a Greek vase or a slow movement by Mozart, is a most worthy and moral aim; if beauty is in your head, if even a fragment of perfection abides in you, it acts as a standard to which you may constantly refer, even if the reference is subconscious. The lines of the vase, the lines of the music – they are a corrective to excess.

So it was with those chairs. They were, of their kind, perfect. And I vowed that never, while I had any say in the matter – and I proposed to have quite a considerable say for quite a considerable time – would I allow anything else into this room which would not be worthy of them. Naturally, they would always be supreme; they would always be the aristocrats. But when other, humbler things came to join them, like poor relations, at least I would make sure that they were gentlemen.

That is what I mean by saying that those chairs changed my life, and continue to change it, to this day.

§ I V

It is arguable that ownership, in matters of taste, is nine-tenths of education. If you possess even one beautiful object it teaches you more, by its constant proximity, than a hundred visits to museums. It is the same with babies, if you understand me. You can hold a great many opinions about babies, if you are unmarried; you can write about babies and lecture about babies *ad infinitum*. Many learned ladies do, laying down the law to their own satisfaction. To me, their opinions are shallow and worthless. I remain obstinately convinced that the only way to know anything about babies is to have one.

So it was with my chairs. For instance, their date – 1695 – became all of a sudden intensely significant; it gave me solid ground to stand on; it was a vantage point from which I could begin to trace the past and to scan the future. They were both there, mutely eloquent in the carved walnut. In the elaborate scroll-work I could discover the lingering riches of the Restoration, in the simple curves of the backs I could see fore-shadowed the approaching elegance of Queen Anne. In the use of the shell motif I could look forward to Sheraton, nearly a hundred stormy years ahead. All sorts of traditions and developments which had hitherto been meaningless suddenly began to make sense, to fall into line, to form themselves into a pattern of coherence and of beauty.

So it was with their maker, Daniel Marot himself. This name, which I had never even heard before, began to crop up in my life, again and again, in the most unexpected circum-stances. It happened that shortly after the arrival of my chairs, I had to make a flying visit to Holland. As I was walk-ing down a street in The Hague, I noticed across the street a very beautiful doorway in carved stone. Something seemed to call me; I crossed over, and stared up at it. The door was open – it was some sort of public building. I stepped inside. Before me rose a stairway of enchanting grace; it seemed to sing its way aloft, in an airy fantasy of marble and painted wood; to walk up those steps, one felt, would be like floating on a cloud.

A nice old guide approached me.

'You are admiring our staircase, sir?'

'Indeed I am.'

He nodded. 'It is one of Daniel Marot's masterpieces,' he said.

And he told me how throughout the length and breadth of Holland there were monuments of Marot's genius – halls and churches and altar-pieces, statues and vases and fountains – all wrought by this man whose very name, a short time ago, was unknown to me.

But it was Marius, as usual, who supplied the final details which enabled me to form a picture, however shadowy, of this elusive genius. Spring was in the air before I saw him again, and by that time the chairs had one or two other pieces to keep them company – a small Hepplewhite settee, a Chippendale tripod table and a Bokhara rug. The settee was shabby, the table was wobbly, and the rug was faded, but they were all gentlemen . . . or ladies, if you prefer it. They might have seen better days, but they could be trusted not to misconduct themselves.

Marius strolled over to the Chippendale table and stroked it affectionately.

'It's all right, isn't it?' I asked the question with some trepidation, because I had bought the table very cheaply.

'Why ask me? I am completely ignorant about furniture.'

'But it is Chippendale, isn't it?'

'I am completely ignorant about Chippendale, too. And likely to remain so.'

'Doesn't he appeal to you?'

'You misunderstand me. Of course he appeals to me. Enormously. He was one of the great figures of English history. The reason I know nothing about him is . . . well . . . the same reason that *you* know nothing about him.'

'And what is that?'

'That there is nothing whatever to know.' He smiled at me quizzically. 'Have you ever seen a picture of Chippendale?'

'No.'

'Or heard a single story about him?'

'No.'

'Or read a single comment on his character?'

'No.'

'Yet you know your eighteenth century. And you've read your Horace Walpole. Of course you have. Well, Walpole was the biggest gossip the world has ever known. He adored poking round people's houses and passing comments on the tiniest details. He must have sat on hundreds of Chippendale chairs. He must have stayed in dozens of great houses when Chippendale was in and out, bustling from room to room, discussing his designs with the owners. He must have been tremendously excited by all that Chippendale was doing. But he never breathed a word about him – not a whisper. Nor did anybody else who came in contact with Chippendale. For all that history has to tell us about him, he might have been invisible.'

'It's incredible. There must be *something* we know about him.'

'Just about as much as we know about Shakespeare. A signature. A few bills. Oh yes – and a fire at his workshop. And then death, at the age of sixty-two. I find it a most intriguing mystery. If there's one thing more fascinating than finding things out, it's *not* finding things out. Don't you think?'

'No, Marius, quite frankly I don't. I'd like to know a lot about Chippendale. Even more, I'd like to know a lot about Marot.'

'Ah yes . . . Marot.'

'Have you found out anything about him?'

Marius did not answer for a moment. He strolled over to one of the chairs, and stood there staring at it, with a little smile on his face – a smile of affection, as though he were greeting an old friend. 'Yes,' he murmured to himself, nodding his head, 'there's no doubt about it. None whatever.' Then he turned back to me. 'Yes. I have found out a little.'

'Tell me.'

'When I went away after our last meeting, I could not get his name out of my head. It kept floating through my memory in the most provoking manner. Apart from that, I was haunted by the chairs themselves. I had a strange feeling that somewhere, at some time, I had seen that design before. And then, I went down to Hampton Court, on business.'

'How can one go to Hampton Court on business?'

'In my ridiculous profession,' retorted Marius 'one can go to the bottom of the sea on business. If it is of any interest, I went to Hampton Court in order to have the right setting for a very delicate conversation with an important lady from Roumania.'

'Go on.'

'We wandered by chance into the Queen's Gallery. It is one of the most beautiful parts of the whole palace, and it is therefore fairly safe to assume that it will always be deserted. I led my Roumanian lady past the immense Delft vases that decorate the chamber. And then I stopped. For there, on one of the vases, was the back of your chair. It was the identical design, drawn in the form of a border to frame the picture of a peacock. And suddenly it all came back to me. It began, of course, with the Edict of Nantes.'

'Marius, you make me feel like Doctor Watson.'

'Only because you *like* feeling like Doctor Watson. It is quite simple. It is merely a matter of dates and deduction.'

'At both of which I am a half-wit.'

'Well, even *you* know what happened in 1685,' said Marius severely. I muttered 'Edict of Nantes', hoping it was right, which it apparently was. 'And even *you* know what happened as a result of that edict.'

By a remote chance I did. It was such a very modern edict. Stalin might have composed it, or Hitler, or any of the other wild beasts who have snarled their way to power in this gracious age.

'And even you,' continued Marius, in a remorseless tone, 'must realize that Marot is a French name. Well, here is a Frenchman, working for William III a few years after the Edict of Nantes. Isn't it obvious that he fled from France to Holland? And that when the Prince of Orange became the King of England, and built the new palace at Hampton Court, Marot came to England with him? And that . . .'

But here I will draw a line, leaving Marius and Marot and me to our own devices. I am all too conscious that the last few pages may have been a dreadful bore. Four walnut chairs, and a tedious, fluttering search for the ghost of the man who fashioned them!

But may I make a last desperate effort to recapture your attention? This man Marot . . . he meant nothing to me, and unless you are a a very specialized sort of connoisseur he probably meant nothing to you. But he was a genius, he really was. There was a divine rhythm in his fingers, and a blessed grace in his mind; and just because of the fact that he happened to be born, to live and breathe and suffer, the world is a more beautiful place. I don't know where his ashes lie, but presumably they lie somewhere. And if you believe, as I do, that in all ashes there is the germ of life, if you share my fancy that every grave, however remote or obscure, is never quite deserted, and that even if the grasses have grown thick around it, they sometimes bear the print of visiting footsteps, however faint or humble . . . then maybe you will hope with me that somewhere, far away, these words may bring a little glow to a handful of dust. It must be pleasant, I think, to be kindly spoken of, even after one is dead.

CHAPTER NINE

PICTURE GALLERY

IF I were ever to marry, and to have a son, I should be impatient for the first day when I could take him to see some great pictures – to tell him why they are wonderful, why they are to be worshipped, and why they are among the works of God.

Where I should begin is any man's guess. Probably at the National Gallery, in front of the Annunciation by Piero della Francesca; for of all the works of man that have flowered throughout the centuries, since the Renaissance, this is one of the rarest. It has the freshness of eternal spring. There is dew in the paint.

I can see my small offspring standing there, clutching my hand, while I try to explain to him what it is all about, why the gold of the virgin's halo is true gold, newly minted, why the miraculous sky is so clearly a gateway to heaven. A formidable task!

And in all probability a fruitless one. Judging by the children who are being sired by one's more artistic friends, one's own son would be inspired by a passion for the comics.

However, it is pleasant to dream – pleasant, but a little sad. For it was not till I came to Merry Hall that I realized the depth of my ignorance of the visual arts, that I knew how many precious years had been wasted. I was not ashamed of my equipment in literature, nor in music, nor even in architecture. But though I had walked through many miles of galleries all over the world, and had paid dutiful visits to the greatest masterpieces, they had not become part of me, they had not aroused the sort of passion that makes a man ache to possess them, or a fragment of them, even if it is only the slightest of sketches from the hand of a master. I had never bought a picture, ancient or modern, in my life. That is a very shaming confession from any man who could have afforded to do so.

Perhaps this was due, in part, to the circumstances of my childhood.

I was brought up surrounded by junk. It was no fault of my mother's, who had an exquisite, natural taste; it was merely a question of money. We had a large house, a quantity of hideous inherited furniture, and an abundance of positively frightening pictures. We had to put up with them.

Half of these things should have been sent up to the attics, but this would not have pleased my father, who liked crowded rooms. Indeed, he constantly added to the chaos by making visits to the junk shops of Torquay, whence he would return, bearing under his arm a tattered painting in oils, usually a portrait in the style of the eighteenth century. This he would prop up in the hall, and invite us to admire it.

'Thirty shillings!' he would exclaim. 'Why, the frame alone is worth that!'

'But it's such a very *ugly* picture,' my mother would murmur.

'Ugly? What's ugly about it? Look at her wig! Look at her necklace! Look at the great house in the background! She's

136

obviously somebody of importance. I shall make her one of the family!'

'Oh dear! Not another?'

'Certainly. This lady is . . . let me see.' Here he would pause, and give a mischievous wink. 'This lady is your great-great-grandmother. Or should it be great-great-great? Yes, three greats I think. And she will hang in the billiards-room, next to my great-great-great-uncle, Sir Thomas.' (Sir Thomas, I should explain, was another junk shop acquisition.) 'I shall call her Louisa. The *Honourable* Louisa.'

So up went the honourable Louisa. And since I was a child, and had no standards of judgment, I accepted the Honourable Louisa, not only as an ancestor of noble birth, but as a painting of noble design. If I did not like it – if I thought the colours murky and the drawing at fault – that must be my own ignorance. Even to this day, when I am studying a master-piece for the first time, I have to blink away a ghostly shadow of the Honourable Louisa.

§ 11

But now a picture was drawing near, drifting towards me, born on the fickle tide of circumstance, whose strange eddies rule our lives. If a certain old lady had not swallowed a fish-bone in a Queen Anne house in Hampstead, that picture would never have come into my life. The eddies would have swept it away to other shores. As it was, she did. And since I have a deep and tender regard for old ladies who swallow fish-bones in Queen Anne houses – (it belonged to a *sole Colbert* which her cook prepared to perfection) – I took her some flowers. She was too ill to see me; I was early for the next appointment, so I decided to walk around and look at the shops.

It was a dismal winter evening, so cold that the gaunt plane trees seemed to shiver in the lamplight; the air was flavoured with the sour spices of an approaching fog. I turned out of a mews into the main street, treading carefully to avoid the puddles in the uneven pavements, and then, on the other side of the road, I saw a patch of blue.

There are times when one's desire for blue is so intense that it must resemble the craving of the drunkard for a glass of whisky. Times when one longs to stretch up and up into the heavens, to wrench away the grey casing of cloud that so often imprisons us, to let loose the floods of colour which are glowing behind. This was one of those times.

I crossed the street, and pressed my nose against the window. Even as I did so, I knew that I was lost. For the blue was shining from the sky and the water of a picture by Canaletto; it seemed to seep through the glass and creep around my heart. I knew that however long I lived, however cold and desolate the ways my feet might wander, this picture held something that I desperately needed. It sang of summer and the South; even in this sombre setting, through the tear-laden glass, it had the sparkle of a carnival.

It was – as I now know – an 'unimportant' picture. A connoisseur would have given it a tolerant smile, murmured 'quite pretty' and passed on. The subject was one which you can see in a hundred galleries all over the world. It showed a stretch of the Grand Canal in Venice, with the Santa Maria di Salute in the background; the azure waters were dotted with gondolas and fishing craft, plying their trade; and closer to hand was the quay of the Riva di Schiavoni, crowded with figures . . . elegant women in masks, courtiers in cloaks of green and scarlet, beggars, flower-women, children with hoops, and several most endearing dogs . . . which, I was happy to observe, looked quite fat. If the dogs had been thin, I should probably never have considered the picture, for most of my travels in Europe have been haunted by starving dogs and cats. I am not very good at going into ecstasies about the proportions of baroque fountains when starving puppies are lying in their shadows.

But the dogs in this picture were obviously well nourished and in the best of spirits. One could gaze at them – and the crowds that surrounded them, and the blue waters, and the flower-women and the cloaked courtiers – without any sinkings of the heart, and without the depressing feeling that one would shortly find oneself walking up some stinking alley, buying sausage meat for them, and generally making oneself a hell of a nuisance to one's companions, whose contemplation of baroque fountains always seems to be disturbed by such conduct.

Venice – summer – the South – the eighteenth century – the scent of the Mediterranean . . . AND large, fat dogs . . . the combination was irresistible.

I opened the door and walked inside.

For a moment nothing happened. And then from the back crept a thin dark man who was the nearest approach to a spider that can ever have emerged in human shape. He had jet black hair, which almost met his eyebrows, boot-button eyes, and thin gangling arms and legs. The only thing which was not spidery about him was his nose, which he appeared to have borrowed from an accommodating vulture.

'Is that a Canaletto in the window?'

'It is the *school* of Canaletto,' hissed the spider.

'May I see it please?'

The spider regarded me intently for a moment; he was presumably deciding the precise position I was to occupy in his web. Then he said, 'Of course.' He fetched the picture and set it on a chair under the light.

'The *school* of Canaletto,' he repeated, gazing at the picture with his head on one side.

'One can see at once that it isn't a genuine Canaletto,' I observed coldly, and instantly hated myself for having said it. Apart from the fact that it was a black lie – for I was quite incompetent to express an opinion – it seemed so very unkind to all concerned. To the courtiers, and the flower-women, and the gondoliers. It was as though I had accused them of being out of drawing. Unkind to the dogs too; unkindest of all to the artist, whoever he was, who had painted it. Somewhere, maybe, I had caused a chilly gust of wind to blow over an Italian grave.

The spider shrugged. 'One can also see that it is a genuine eighteenth-century picture. I am prepared to give you a guarantee to that effect.'

'It is certainly very pretty,' I admitted, brushing away a small piece of web which had unaccountably got into my hair.

'Is it not?' The spider moved a step closer. 'I cannot believe that there is *anybody* who would not like such a picture. It smiles at you.'

'It does indeed. May I ask how much it is?'

There was a momentary pause. Then he named a figure.

'Oh dear!'

'Is that too much?'

The spider would have been surprised if I had told him that, on the contrary, it was too little. If it had been more, I should have broken free from his web – which was now beginning to twine round my left ankle – and have escaped into the night. But the sum he had mentioned could just be contrived.

'I shall have to think it over.'

'For cash,' insisted the spider – and I could not help wondering whether all this webbing was being produced through his nostrils, or from the tips of his fingers, or even from the region of his navel – 'for cash I might consider a *small* reduction.'

I repeated that I would think it over, took his card, and beat a retreat. Spectral strands of web trailed after me down the foggy street.

Next day, the picture was mine.

§ I I I

Of course, it had to go in the drawing-room, where it was welcomed by the Marot chairs which – though they did not precisely rise and bow to it – were obviously delighted to be joined by such elegant company.

And of course, it had to be hung over the fireplace, which meant, almost immediately, more appalling expense. For the ugly angular mantlepiece had to be pulled down, and replaced by one of carved wood, with swags of fruit and flowers, and two most endearing griffons putting their tongues out, not in any spirit of discourtesy but from sheer *joie de vivre*.

And of course there had to be a striplight under it, and a little plaque announcing that it was 'School of Canaletto'. This gave me a feeling of immense importance. To own a picture worthy of being lit and labelled – this is a miracle that can only be appreciated by those whose entire youth was spent, as was mine, surrounded by bogus ancestors and fly-blown reproductions of engravings by Marcus Stone.

And, of course, it proved to be yet another distracting influence, keeping me from work. Small and very special bunches of flowers had to be picked for it, only to be discarded, for it did not seem to need flowers in its neighbourhood. The only floral competition it will tolerate is a bowl of gentians, or a few deep blue violets. It had to be kept out of draughts – and if you think that I am being 'whimsical' you would be, for once in a way, mistaken; old pictures cannot abide draughts, nor, for that matter, any extreme of heat or cold. And it had to be visited, and gloated over, at all hours of the day and night. I could not feel happy until I was personally acquainted with every figure on the crowded canvas, from the scruffiest fisher-boy to the smallest child framed in the most distant balcony. As there were nearly a hundred figures, it was a lengthy process.

But it was worth it. Every hour with that picture has been

an hour of peace, like a little holiday. It is beautiful at all times, but if I had to name any moment when it is most vividly alive, I would choose the hour of sunset, when the last light creeps across the western fields, through the tall poplars, over the low hedge of the lane, till it glides through my window, illuminating the gilt of the old frame, and slowly spreading over the expectant canvas. It is as though all Venice – my patch of Venice – were waiting for this moment. The first shaft of light always shines on the dome of the Santa Maria di Salute, and then spreads along the clouds behind it, so that their edges are flushed with gold. Even as you are staring at these painted clouds, which are no longer painted, but have become in fact real clouds, blowing and billowing, you notice that another finger of light is pointing to a patch of water beneath a gondola, and is causing it to sparkle, to become translucent, so that you could swear that you can suddenly see in it the reflection of the scarlet cap of the gondolier . . . a reflection which was not there a moment ago. And surely the gondolier himself is growing in stature? You can see his muscles swelling beneath his blue jersey, and if you look very closely you realize that though his head is turned, there must be a smile on his face. Indeed, the whole picture has begun to smile. The sun has spread delight over the surface of the waters, there is laughter in every ripple of Chinese white, there is gaiety and movement in the swirl of every painted cloak that struts the waterfront.

On a windy April evening, when the skies are wet and gleaming, when the sun shines fitfully, and the poplars bend and shimmer against the sunset, so that the whole room is a kaleidoscope of shifting lights, then the miracle of the Canaletto is at its height. I do not expect you to believe me, but I swear that in the stormy English twilight the picture is alive, that it strains to escape from its frame, and that in the ancient canvas the clouds race across the sky, the sails tug at their masts, and the foam is blown across the mimic lagoon. I should not be in the least surprised if one evening I were to come in and find. on the neighbouring wall, some specks of Venetian salt.

§ I V

My little gallery will not delay us overlong; its walls are still mostly bare; and the few pictures which hang there have nothing in common except the love that assembled them.

My next acquisition was a Patrick Nasmyth. If you have never heard of Patrick Nasmyth, that need not embarrass you; neither had I, before this picture was mine. Yet we should have heard of him; he has hung in the National Gallery for many years. He might be described as a minor Constable, and not so minor as all that, for at times he painted with a brilliance which even Constable might have envied. One of those times was when he painted my picture. It shows a country road, bending down-hill, deeply shadowed with trees, very English trees, oak and elm and ash and elderberry. A man is walking down the road, away from us, with two dogs roaming in front of him – a black dog and a white dog – drawn with extreme economy, but so skilfully that you can almost hear them sniff. On the left is a latticed cottage, with a white gate, at which a man with a red face is standing, beckoning to the figure who is walking away from us.

And then, as we look ahead, there is a burst of poetry. Field after field, stretching into the far distance, fold upon fold, green upon green, ending in a line of grey so delicate, so miraculous, that you can hardly believe it was painted by a human hand. Just a few inches of canvas, but all England is in that tiny passage. If you had a magic glass, and could enlarge the picture a thousand times, you would find wild roses growing in the hedgerows and startle the blackbirds from the coppices.

Once again it was Marius who brought this artist to life for me. Nasmyth was, of course, in all the major works of reference, but they gave scant information beyond the dates of his birth and death, and the various galleries in which his work had been collected. Marius clothed these dry bones with flesh.

When I first showed him the picture he stared at it for a long time without speaking.

'What are you thinking, Marius?'

'I was thinking how very unfortunate it was that more artists do not learn to paint with the left hand.'

'But did Nasmyth paint with his left hand?'

He flicked his fingers impatiently. 'People who are so ignorant do not deserve to own beautiful pictures at all. Of course he painted with his left hand. His right was hopelessly maimed when he was a boy.'

I stared again at the picture. It seemed even more wonderful than before.

'He also slept in a damp bed,' snapped Marius. 'I suppose you will tell me that you were unaware of *that?*'

'By a curious chance I was. But I don't see what that has got to do with my picture.'

'It has everything to do with it. Because he slept in a damp bed he contracted a rare illness – your ignorance must be infectious because I cannot recall the name of it – which resulted in deafness. Because he was deaf he was solitary, and because he was solitary he began to drink. He fell into what are known as "bad habits", and the company he kept was very low. He even preferred his friends to have some physical deformity; he cultivated cripples and hunchbacks; I suppose he felt on terms of equality with them. Now I come to think of it, you can even see a trace of that in his pictures.'

'How?'

He pointed to a group of trees. 'He's stunted those trees. They're dwarfed. The limbs are contorted.'

'They're still very beautiful.' I was not sure whether I liked my trees to be called deformities.

'I did not suggest that they were not. I was merely offering a few elementary hints that might help you to appreciate a picture which, as I said before, you do not deserve to possess.'

Marius spoke quite tartly, and volunteered no more information, beyond the fact that Nasmyth died at Lambeth in August 1831.

'It was during a very fierce thunderstorm,' he added. 'They propped him up in bed so that he could watch it.'

Whenever there is a thunderstorm at Merry Hall I go and stand near the Patrick Nasmyth. If it is at night, the lightning flashes through the window, illuminating the canvas for a split second of beauty. And I find myself dreaming about the sad young man who painted it, and wondering whether perhaps he may be somewhere near me, in the heart of the storm.

§ v

Three more pictures, and we shall have done.

The first cost £15 including the frame. I bought it from a London dealer whose name is Peter Claas. Peter, I fear, is doomed to failure in the world of art, for three excellent reasons; he is a gentleman, he is completely honest, and he has exquisite taste. Such handicaps, in such a profession, are almost insurmountable.

Peter suspected that it might be from the hand of a master – or, at least, a minor master. It was a self-portrait of a young man of remarkable beauty. He was wearing a classical robe; in his hand was a drawing tablet, and he was turning his head as though regarding himself in a mirror. The whole work was in various delicate tones of sepia, and underneath was the inscription:

K   L.S.   145

LAUGHTER ON THE STAIRS

JOHANNES ANTICUS
GRONINGA
HANC SUAM EFFIGIEM PINGIT ROMA MDCCXXXVI
AET ANN XXX

Perhaps other people's Latin was even worse than mine; perhaps nobody else had realized that Anticus must be a Latinization of the name of the artist; perhaps nobody had bothered to look him up. I did so, with the happiest results. Johannes Antiquus proved to be indeed a minor master. Born at Groningen in 1706, he had won European fame by the time he painted my picture. He had been hung in the Academy at Florence, had found a patron in the Grand Duke of Tuscany, and had been fêted by the Prince of Orange in the Palace of Loo, where he painted a large picture of 'Mars disarmed by the Graces'. He must feel that it is rather a come-down to be hung in Merry Hall, but I hope he likes to be remembered.

He must surely be flattered by the attentions of Our Rose, who often stands before him, and sighs, and murmurs. . . .

'If only he could *speak!*'

It is perhaps lucky that he cannot do so, for I suspect that he would only tell her to go away.

Anybody who does not adore my next picture should have his or her head examined, and if that does not have any effect, should put it in the oven. It is a very early seventeenth-century landscape by Roelandt Savery. It was painted about thirty years after Shakespeare wrote *A Midsummer Night's Dream*, which might well have inspired it. Through the thick branches of an enchanted wood a distant landscape glimmers in the twilight; in the foreground Orpheus and Eurydice are entwined; and the whole design is a miracle of golden leaves and silver shadows.

I shall 'do a Marius' with regard to Savery, and assume that you know all about him. Since he hangs in most of the great galleries of Europe, the assumption is not too preposterous. At

146

the same time, I confess – if it is any comfort – that I had
never heard of him myself till this picture came my way.

§ V I

But I had heard, of course, of Pannini – the last picture in
our little gallery. Only too often had I heard of him. For
almost anybody can own a 'Pannini' in inverted commas. All
that is needed is a trusting nature, a bleak ignorance of the
elements of art, and a small sum of money, varying from ten
to fifty pounds.

With these endowments you may purchase three square
feet of classical ruins lurking in a fog of dirty varnish. Perched
among these ruins, in flowing draperies, will be various figures
whose limbs are so ill-drawn that they appear to be suffering
from a painful tropical disease. In the top left hand corner will
be a patch of muddy blue, while the rest of the background is
obscured by flocks of angry clouds. Angry, as well they might
be, at being painted so badly.

There are thousands of these 'Pannini's' hanging on the
walls of English houses. They have been purchased by people
who ought to know better, and sometimes do. Such people
want the prestige of art without the painful necessity of paying
for it. They see the three square feet of pretentious, murky
canvas and they say to themselves: 'Really, that would look
quite impressive in the hall; it has a label on it too – Pannini –
well I never! I'm sure I've heard that name before; he must
be an old master.' Then they say to themselves that if they
had an old master it would be quite enraging for Mrs. Jones,
when next she came to tea. The thought of enraging Mrs.
Jones, and setting up as connoisseurs of art is too much for
them, so they plonk down their ten to fifty pounds, and take
the thing away in a taxi.

Fortunately they seldom have it cleaned. If they did, the
aforesaid victims of elephantiasis, lurking among the ruins,

would shine out in such a horrid light that they would be obliged to turn its face to the wall.

Whenever I see these 'Pannini's' I grind my teeth. If their owners refer to them, as they usually do, with a wave of the hand and a casual 'Rather a good Pannini, I'm told', I turn on them such a ghastly grin that they hastily change the subject. Which is just as well, for if I were really to say what I thought, it would be very rude indeed. I should say: 'You do not offer me rancid fish paste and call it caviar. You do not open a bottle of cheap cider and ask me to have a glass of champagne. You do not introduce me to a blend of bulldog and cocker spaniel and refer to it as a prize Borzoi. (I should much prefer the blend, but that is beside the point.) So why do you do these things in the name of art?'

A genuine Pannini, of the best period – the middle of the eighteenth century – is worthy to hang by the side of the great masters. He was a romantic of the Roman ruins; he thought ruins, dreamed ruins, and created ruins all his life, and these ruins he peopled with entrancing youths and maidens who appear to enjoy them almost as much as he obviously did himself. For paradoxically enough, there is a spirit of delight in the midst of all this destruction; the ruins evoke no melancholy meditations, they merely form a gay and rhythmical design. One has the feeling that if Pannini had ever been required to paint a building that was in perfect condition, he would have felt quite unhappy about it, and would have inquired, rather plaintively, whether it were not possible to knock down a few pillars, or at least, to blast a hole in the roof.

I am sitting beneath the Pannini as I write. It is a large picture, a Roman scene, and it is chock-a-block with ruins – fallen pillars, cracked façades, crumbling staircases, mouldering statues. It is all as happy as a sandboy. Like most true examples of the work of this master, it has a silver quality, a delicate *patine*; every cloud has a silver lining. And though the figures grouped so gracefully among the fallen masonry are rosy and glowing in the sunlight, there is silver in their veins and even a touch of silver in their hair. The sun shines golden on the great marble columns that tower into the blue, but here again it drops hints of silver, in the tracery of the acanthus leaves that curve up the Corinthian capitals; and in the branches of the trees that hang in the background, like a cool tapestry of green, there are silver shadows.

Just as the Canaletto is a picture of the sunset, so the Pannini is a picture of the morning. Every day, when I come downstairs, I open the door of the drawing-room, and walk inside, and stand in front of it. Whether the light from the eastern windows is the golden sunshine of June or the grey mist of November, whether there is frost or fog or storm or cloud, the Pannini shines with a silver radiance. I climb over all the rocks, and jump from one fallen column to another. A Pannini, you will observe, is good for the figure. Not only because it makes you take all this mental exercise, but because the young men in it are so perfectly proportioned, so straight and god-like, that you find yourself comparing their shapes with your own. Then you begin to wonder. And if ever the day were to come when you were to glance down and observe in yourself the beginning of a middle-aged spread, you would, I hope, do something about it.

So there we are, at the end of the gallery, and I fear that for many of you it must all have been a dreadful bore. But you must remember, *mes enfants*, that it is sometimes very good for you to be bored. Boredom is the beginning of know-ledge, and knowledge is the beginning of taste. There are many weary roads to travel, many perilous cliffs to climb, before one reaches these rare uplands where one can study the work of the masters in a true light, and with a clean eye. I have still a long, long way to travel, the clouds of ignorance are still thick about me, but sometimes they clear, and I see. I have taken the first stumbling steps towards the high temple. If any of you are still by my side, I shall be flattered.

CHAPTER TEN

BIRD SONG

THERE are so many miracles happening all the year round at Merry Hall – or, for that matter, in any country house – that I spend half my life gaping. During the winter it is bad enough; even the silver lace that the frost hangs on the window-panes overnight is enough to make one get out of bed dancing the fandango. But in the spring it is almost unbearable, for then the curtain goes up at 4 a.m. to a Hallelujah chorus of the birds. When the birds sing Hallelujah it is only common decency to sing Hallelujah too. You cannot do that lying on your back in bed, staring at the ceiling. You have to do it outside, on the lawn, with your bare feet in the dew.

This fourth spring I went bird's-nesting, by which I do not mean crashing like a bison through the bushes, wrecking other people's houses. It was a question of watching, and listening, and, when the time came, of standing and staring. For the miracle of a bird's nest is almost the greatest miracle of all.

Think of it like this. . . .

An aery meeting, a flutter of feathers and then, before you know where you are, a beautiful house, perched in the branches of a tree.

That is only the beginning of it.

Shortly, on the floor of the house, exquisite ornaments are deposited by unseen hands. These ornaments are light blue, or pale green, or speckled like a fritillary; they are oval in shape, and fashioned from the most delicate, fragile porcelain.

Even then the miracle has only just begun.

For each of these ornaments contains music.

Liquid music, sleeping music, disguised in the form of two magic fluids, one gold and one white. Unwritten music, as yet, but music which one day will echo through the woods like distant flutes.

If you were to write this in the guise of a fairy story, even the most amiable child would suggest that you were straining his credulity. 'It's all very well saying the magician did all that with his wand,' he would say, 'but really, there are limits. Houses in trees, blue ornaments filled with music, and music disguised in the form of magic fluids . . . it's altogether too complicated. Can't you make him do something simple and obvious, like changing Auntie into an ant-eater?'

And yet, what is there in the foregoing description which is not the sober truth about the nest of the commonest thrush? There *is* an 'aery meeting', and as a result of that meeting there is a house in a tree. Ornaments *are* laid on the floor of that house, for if you do not think that thrushes' eggs are ornamental, then either you must have a collection of quite exceptional jade, or your taste must run to rows of small ebony elephants, glaring at each other's behinds.

These ornaments *are* filled with unwritten music. It is all there, 'tuning up'. There is the white and there is the yolk, and between the two of them there will one day be a bird, with a swelling throat and an eager heart, singing for you and me.

You may tell me that you could rhapsodize, in the same way, about the embryo of a baby. Perhaps you could. I couldn't. Having babies is in no way to be compared with depositing delicate pieces of porcelain in the branches of cherry trees. It is a far less decorative process. Whether it is a more useful one is open to question.

However that may be, I went bird's-nesting. In this pursuit I was lucky to have the company of Miss Mint.

§ 11

Miss Mint had thoroughly settled into our little community. The only person who ever said a word against her was Erica Wyman, who constantly complained that she had been over-charged for 'Caravan'.

'Four thousand pounds was quite ridiculous,' she said to Our Rose. 'There's been a terrible slump in Tudor cottages.'

'Miss Mint could hardly have been expected to know that.'

'A terrible slump,' repeated Erica, ignoring her. 'And I don't wonder. I have a permanent headache, bumping into those beams.'

'I should have thought that you would have been used to stooping after all those years in a caravan.'

'I shall have to lower the floors. And a pretty penny *that* will cost.'

'You will have to economize, dear,' suggested Rose. 'Or perhaps you could take in a paying guest?'

What Erica would have said, and what action she would have taken, if her well had dried up, nobody can tell. But it remained full to the brim. The ways of wells, as all will agree who have ever owned one, are quite incalculable.

Meanwhile Miss Mint, unaware af even a shadow of dis-cord, moved happily among us. She was still the most timid of creatures, and the mystic letters N.W.H. still appeared on

the envelopes of all her letters, but she was enjoying life. Whenever she came to Merry Hall she bore with her a little gift, usually something she had made herself – a pot of wild strawberry jam, or some of her special pickled walnuts, or a small bag of her own recipe for pot pourri. But the best thing she brought was herself. It would be too fanciful to suggest that the birds sang more sweetly when she was around; she merely taught me how to listen to them. To listen, not only with a vague pleasure, but with the intelligence and knowledge that are the foundations of true delight. By doing so, she brought a new savour into my life.

January and February, in the old days, had meant the rosy glow of the winter heathers, the first chill blossoms of the hellebore, and the exotic delicacy of the *iris stylosa*. Now it had an added significance; I listened for the robins beginning to chirrup, and the sparrows to twitter in the eaves; and I knew that if I was lucky, on a day that was not so cold, I could hear a skylark, high above the stubble fields.

March had been a matter of searching for the early wood anemones, sniffing the pink buds of the daphnes, gathering sprays of wintersweet and winter honeysuckle. Now there were other excitements. Miss Mint showed me where the blackbirds were nesting in the shrubbery, and the rooks in the elms, and when we went our walks together, told me how to tell the curious, impertinent note of the pied wagtail.

April had meant dog violets and primroses, blackthorn blooming and early cowslips. But now the whole sky was alive with birds, flocking to the English spring; the celestial highways were chock-a-block, with swallows in the vanguard, closely followed by the willow warblers – (who do, oddly enough, warble in willows) – with cuckoos and swifts and sand martins and heaven knows what else. And of course, bringing up the rear, at a short distance from the common crowd, the nightingales. I always like to think that the nightingales are the last birds to arrive, like prima donnas who take their leisure, and

evade the jostling of the common crowd. Miss Mint tells me
that there are several birds who come later, the wood warblers
and the nightjars among them. Perhaps she is right. She
usually is. However, the nightingales are *almost* the last, and
do not begin their solo arias until there has been a great deal of
preliminary chorus work on the part of the minor artistes.

§ I I I

'I often think,' Miss Mint once said to me, 'that people talk
more nonsense about the habits of birds than about any other
subject. Perhaps it is because we can't fly, and follow them.
We just stay on the ground, and see strange things happening
overhead, and we draw our own conclusions, which are usually
ridiculous. Even Doctor Johnson talked nonsense about
birds!'

This was indeed a revolutionary statement from Miss Mint;
in her veneration for Doctor Johnson she vied with Cranford's Miss Jenkins. Boswell stood next to *Daily Light* by her
bedside.

'Yes indeed,' she went on. 'He really believed that swallows
spend the winter under water, on the beds of ponds and
rivers.'

'How could he believe such a thing?'

'It was what they call "common knowledge" at the time.
And as he was a Londoner, with no opportunity to check the
facts, I suppose he just accepted the legend. So *very* unlike
him! I don't think I should have remembered the passage
if it had not been for a certain word.'

'What word was that?'

'Conglobulate.' Miss Mint twittered softly. 'Such a nice,
round, cosy word. He said the swallows "conglobulated
together", flying round and round in a sort of heap, and that
then they all threw themselves into the water.'

Conglobulate! It was indeed a pleasing phrase. I wondered what would happen if I wrote to Our Rose and suggested that she might come round one evening for a spot of conglobulation. I had a feeling that she would not be amused.

One of Miss Mint's favourite birds is the robin, and it was not long before I was able to introduce her to my own particular robin, whose name is Ernest. He was given that name because he first came into my life a few days after I had witnessed a specially sparkling performance of *The Importance of Being Earnest*; and as he perched on the barrow I was reminded of The Importance of Being Robin. It is indeed important, if you are a bird. Robins, as Miss Mint told me, are protected from human persecution by many ancient superstitions.

'Did you know,' she asked me one day, 'that robins were called God Almighty's birds?'

'No. Why?'

'Because when Jesus was dying on the cross it was a robin who tried to pull out the thorns from His crown. He was just a little brown bird, in those days. But as he fluttered round, trying so hard to be a help, his breast was stained with blood. And God, from that moment, gave all the robins red breasts, all over the world, in honour of that one bird.'

It must be for this reason that such terrible warnings are still given to children, throughout the countryside, against the dangers of stealing from a robin's nest. 'As soon as your arm reaches up to the nest it will wither, and you will never be able to lift it again.' It was a very old woman whom I heard say that, but she believed it, and so did her daughter. And so, most certainly, did her small grandson, who sometimes comes and does a job of weeding. For Ernest is constantly by his side, on these occasions, and has even been known to perch on his cap. He would never do that unless he were sure he was with friends.

§ I V

Listening to bird song, learning to identify the individual notes in the Hallelujah chorus, is not as easy as one might think. Anybody can tell the song of a nightingale or the hoot of an owl. And fortunately there is no other bird, except perhaps the woodpecker, that makes anything approaching the screech of the jay – though the jays look so cheerful, and drop such delicate little feathers on the lawns that I have not the heart to shoo them away. (The first time I found a jay's feather, which is made of turquoise blue silk embroidered with grey and black pearls, it had alighted on a clump of deep blue Canterbury bells. It was early morning; the dew was still heavy; and the tiny drops sparkled over the blue of the feather and the blue of the petals. The effect was of some exquisite piece of jeweller's work, dropped overnight by an elegant but absent-minded fairy.)

But we were saying how difficult it is to identify the notes of the Hallelujah chorus. The reason for this is very simple; it is because birds, as Miss Mint taught me, are such incorrigible mimics. Just when you think that you have heard the song of a bullfinch, and peer around in search of it, you look up and see that it comes from a mischievous starling, winking at you from the lilacs. At the very moment when you think you have finally 'isolated' the twitter of the robin, he will perch by your side and give a perfect imitation of a wren. (I have heard that robins have even been known to mimic the song of the nightingale, but this sounds rather difficult to believe.)

Why birds have this extraordinary faculty is one of the deepest mysteries of nature, and I know of no naturalist who has ever attempted to explain it. What useful purpose, for instance, is served by a perfectly good blackbird pretending to be a rook? Is it giving some mysterious note of warning? Does it imagine that it will gain in social prestige? Does it *want* to be a rook?

Or is it just 'having fun'? To me this explanation is the likeliest of all. We often forget that animals do have fun. We are so obsessed with the 'Nature red in tooth and claw' school of thought that we overlook the fact that nature, very often, wears a broad grin. Elephants gambol, dolphins sport, all the felines indulge in the craziest tricks, out of sheer high spirits. Even crabs, I suspect, must sometimes kick up their heels as they slither over the rocks, and give each other playful nips. 'Life is not all a bloody struggle, all the time.' Tennyson was right, of course, and so was Huxley. But Walt Disney was right, as well.

However that may be, here is a problem of mimicry which some bird-watcher may perhaps be able to solve for me.

I have long been certain that birds like music. If you play the piano with the windows open, at any time during the singing season, there is an immediate response from outside. Of this there is no doubt whatever; it is like the sudden crescendo of tuning-up which goes on in an orchestra as soon as the conductor's head is seen coming out of the orchestra pit. It is particularly noticeable with light, airy music, which contains plenty of arpeggio passages and an abundance of cadenzas.

Yes, the birds certainly like it. But though they were appreciative, I always thought that they were a somewhat indiscriminate audience; it did not seem to matter whether one played well or ill. Until a certain evening in April.

It was towards dusk, when the blackbirds were having heated arguments in the shrubbery – they always seem excited by the fading of the light. I was playing the piano with the windows open. Miss Mint was perched on a stool by the fire. It was something of an occasion, because for the past three months I had been learning that wayward, wandering piece 'The Maiden and the Nightingale', by Granados, and this was the first time that I had played it to an audience. It is not nearly as easy as it sounds. I had endured delicious agonies and tortures, night after night, trying to do trills with my left hand. Gaskin had been driven almost to distraction; the cats had crouched, in terror, under the sofa. And sometimes when I retired, wincing with pain from the elbows downwards, I understood the desperation which Schumann must have felt, when he tied a piece of string above his bed, and attached it to his little finger, which had persistently refused to obey his commands.

At last it was 'coming', and I felt that it could be tried out on Miss Mint, who would not mind if there were wrong notes, or if the trills differed, in some respects, from those of Horowitz.

In case you do not know this piece, I should explain that it is an elaborate and very subtle embroidery of one haunting phrase – a phrase which, in fact, is never finished. The melody rises for a bar, hovers for another bar, falls, and falls again . . . and then, just when you are wondering what it is going to do, it begins again, in another key, sometimes in another tempo. Only a composer of infinite resource could have given to so slight a theme such a sense of richness, of mystery, of echoes within echoes. It has caught all the most poignant quality of bird-song itself.

Well, there I was playing it to Miss Mint. Page one went smoothly enough, for it was merely a series of statements of the theme, written as simply as a plainsong. Then came the first elaboration, with the first trill. Something went wrong; I stopped, and muttered an apology. In the sudden silence there came the song of a bird, repeating the first seven notes.

I stared at Miss Mint.

'Did you hear that?'

'Indeed I did.' She put her fingers to her lips. 'Listen!'

The silence was unbroken.

'Perhaps, if you played it again. . . .'

I played the same passage, with somewhat more force, and great clarity, stopping at the same place.

For a moment nothing happened. Then, again, came those seven notes, perfectly in pitch and in tempo.

Miss Mint had tiptoed to the window, and was looking out. 'It's coming from the lime tree,' she whispered. 'If only there were a little more light we could see what it was.'

'Could it be a thrush?'

She shook her head. 'I don't think so. Wait! There's something along that branch that might be a blackbird . . . but could a blackbird . . . '

She stopped. There it was again. The opening phrase of 'The Maiden and the Nightingale', by Granados, written in the year 1912, in the key of F sharp, price three shillings and sixpence from any respectable music publishers.

We stayed there, hardly daring to breathe, looking out into the growing darkness. But the song had ceased. Then, a moment later, there was a chirrup, and a flutter of wings, and something dark flew out of the lime tree, over to the distant fields.

That is all there is to the story. I wish that somebody could tell me what might be the explanation of it – what strange fragment of ornithological magic I had hit upon. Otherwise, I shall never be able to play that piece properly. 'The Maiden and the Nightingale' will be all mixed up. There will be thrush noises in the bass, and blackbird noises in the treble, and before I know what is happening I shall have drifted into Delius, and find myself giving an impromptu performance of 'On first hearing the Cuckoo in Spring'.

§ V

A great lover of birds who read the foregoing passage – without being able to solve the mystery – said to me 'I cannot understand anybody who loves birds, as you do, being able to keep cats in the house. When I see a cat with a bird in its mouth, I see red.'

It is, I suppose, a bit of a paradox. Whenever one of these grim little tragedies happens in the garden, I see red myself. No, that is not quite the way to put it; anger is a foolish emotion on such occasions; one might as well be angry with an octopus for using the tentacles God gave it. It is rather that I have a feeling of deep distress, of profound *malaise*, as though Nature had suddenly stripped away her lovely mask of flowers, and was grinning at me from a bleeding skull.

Fortunately, my own cats very seldom seem to catch anything at all. Whether this is due to the overwhelming amiability of their master, which seeps into their souls, I am not the one to say. I am afraid that it is just sheer incompetence.

The only thing that 'One' has caught, in the past year, is an enormous dragonfly. In early summer the smooth surface of the lily pond becomes a positive aerodrome of dragon-flies, that swoop in from all points of the compass, in a glitter of silver and peacock blue. 'One' sits watching them, gaping like a small boy who dreams of being a pilot, and from time to time he darts a paw at them through the iris leaves, with no result whatever.

It must have been a very slow dragonfly that he caught, and a very tough one, because it lodged in his mouth and refused to depart. He came wailing to me, in great distress, looking very strange, as though he had luminous whiskers. I removed the dragonfly; it gave its wings a contemptuous flick and then shot out through the open window. The whole episode was like a sequence in a Walt Disney cartoon.

'Five' never catches anything at all except – alas – bees. Although he has been stung by them time and time again, he stalks out to the heather-bed, crouches down in the clumps, with his green eyes gleaming as though he were engaged on some heroic enterprise, and pounces. The result is inevitable. He is stung, usually on the nose. Whereupon the whole household is disorganized for at least an hour, and there are strugglings and dabbings with damp cloths, and heated discussions as to whether the sting is out or whether it isn't. At the end of it all he is put down on the kitchen floor, and we say to him: 'There! Perhaps that will teach you a lesson!' On the next day he starts all over again.

'Four' is the hunter. Not a very successful one, not a very savage one. But hunting is in his blood. It leads to painful scenes between us.

I see him in the distance, sitting on a bank, staring at a hole in the grass. In that hole, as I am only too well aware, is a family of field-mice. They are the most charming of field-mice, diffident, retiring, unobtrusive. Why does 'Four' want to be beastly to them?

I go out to him, and sit down by his side.

' "Four," ' I say, 'this is really rather a waste of time, don't you think?'

No reply.

'You must have been here for at least an hour. Could you not be better employed?'

A shrug, and a flick of the tail.

'There is some delicious fish in the kitchen.' (Even the mention of the fish starts all sorts of moral problems in my brain. Hooks, and gaping mouths. One must become a vegetarian, or have something done to one.)

'And if you want to play with anything,' I continue hastily, 'here is a beautiful dock-leaf, which I will squiggle before you.'

I do so. The dock-leaf is spurned.

So there is nothing to do but to take him up, carry him to the furthest part of the orchard, lift him on to the branches of a pear tree, and walk away, in the hope that by the time he climbs down he will have forgotten about the field-mice, and discover some more innocent diversion.

Strange as it may seem, the cats have helped to contribute to my store of knowledge about the ways of the birds. If it had not been for some suspicious activities on the part of

'Four', near an old briar bush in the coppice, I might never have learned of one of the most fabulous habits of the cuckoo.

'I think there must be a nest in that briar,' I said to Miss Mint one day. 'Shall we go and see?'

So we walked up to the coppice, and on the way through the orchard we found two eggs, lying in the grass. The first was glossy blue, with brown and grey spots, which I recognized as belonging to a thrush.

'What is this egg doing here?' I asked her.

'If I could answer that question I should be quite famous,' she replied. 'Mrs. Thrush is always dropping her eggs at random. Almost as if she did not care for them.'

We walked on. Here was the briar, and here was the second egg. A little greeny-blue egg, which Miss Mint picked up.

'This egg is still warm,' she murmured.

'It looks like a sparrow's. Is it?'

'Yes. A hedge-sparrow's. But they never drop their eggs.' She paused, and peered into the briar, which was very dense. 'Something has been going on.'

My heart sank; it seemed only too obvious what had been going on. 'Four' must be the culprit.

But I was maligning him. At that very moment there was a scurry and a squawk, and out of the bush flew a bird that looked like a small hawk, with a long black tail.

'Well I never!' exclaimed Miss Mint. 'A cuckoo! So that was it!'

She told me that we had caught a cuckoo in the very act of laying its egg in another bird's nest.

The greatest thrill of all was yet to come. We made our way to the nest, which needed a lot of patience, for the briars were sharp and tangled, and we had to move them very carefully to avoid disturbing the nest. At last we were able to peer into it. There, displayed before us, was the miracle of the cuckoo's egg. There were four eggs in the nest, three small, and one not so small. *But all were of precisely the same shade of greeny-blue*. By some strange chemical process which must surely baffle the brain of a Darwin, the eggs that a cuckoo lays are almost always coloured in precisely the same shade, and with precisely the same specks and dots, as the eggs of the bird whose territory she is usurping.

If that is not enough to make one think, and think again, and go on thinking until one feels exceedingly small and insignificant, I don't know what is.

So 'Four', you see, has inadvertently taught me quite a lesson through his wicked habits.

But I cannot grant that they are wicked. Cats and birds – birds and cats – they are all part of a gigantic pattern of conflict and pain and mystery which it is not given us, as yet, to understand. We do not know enough to enable us to take sides in that eternal battle. The more we know, the less we shall feel inclined to do so. Even birds, we must remember, are not all saints. The habits of vultures leave much to be desired, by the standards of polite society. So do the habits of magpies, who will fix on baby rabbits, and subject them to a slow and hideous death by pecking out their eyes.

However, we need not finish this little adventure on so ugly a note. 'Red in tooth and claw' . . . that is understood. But not all the time. Life, for the birds, has a brighter colour, and a happier note. And if you listen to their singing, really listen to it, you will notice one thing about it which is surely significant. No bird ever sings in a minor key.[1]

[1] With the possible exception of the barnowl. And he, poor dear, is always so very flat that he hardly counts.

THERE are, I am told, certain bleak and squalid people to whom the advent of a new kitten is a matter of comparative indifference. Somebody in the household says 'There are mice in the kitchen'. To which somebody else replies, 'Perhaps we'd better get a cat.' A few days later a trembling, ecstatic bundle of fur arrives at the back door, eager to make friends in this strange new world, only to be roughly dumped out of a basket, and left to cower under the kitchen sink. If it ever dares to push its small nose beyond the baize door that leads to the more genteel quarters of the house, it is brusquely shoved away.

Yes, there are indeed people who treat new kittens like that. I have met them, in very grand houses that are usually filled with extremely expensive dogs. One wanders out after luncheon to admire the herbaceous borders – which are enough to make one feel quite sick, anyway, partly with envy at their opulence and partly with disgust at their lack of taste – and there, sheltering behind a clump of delphiniums, is a thin, scared tabby, who has quite obviously never had a kind word said to it in its life. There is only one thing to do on these occasions. One must leave the party, advance towards the tabby, grasp it firmly, and woo it with the various classical movements which are familiar to cat-lovers, beginning, of course, with movement Number One, which consists in firm rhythmical strokes under the chin, in an upward direction. When the tabby has been convinced that at last somebody human has appeared on its sad horizon, and when it is relaxed, and beginning to simmer, one must return to the guests – who will probably be standing on the lawn, staring at this unwonted exhibition with some astonishment – and say how beautiful the tabby is, how much more beautiful it is, indeed, than anything one has seen in the course of the day. (At this point one's eyes should alight on the nearest debutante.) When this has registered, one must continue, in loud and ringing tones, to say how strange it is that it is so THIN, in spite of the care with which one is quite *certain* it must have been treated, in spite of all the adoration which must quite *obviously* have been lavished upon so adorable a creature. This sinister remark must be aimed directly at one's hostess, and if you can back it up by a few hints that one proposes to write, as soon as possible, some lurid and personal revelations in the Sunday papers about rich people who neglect animals, so much the better. One's conduct should have two quite happy results. Firstly, the tabby will get a square meal. Secondly, one will never be asked to luncheon again.

Incidentally, out of the blue, here is a story about Noel Coward and cats, which is so endearing that I will set it down before it is forgotten. One day Noel came to stay at Merry Hall. As I greeted him at the front door I noticed that 'One' had also come to pay his respects, and was standing behind, waiting to be introduced. I was not sure of Noel's position in the feline universe, so I said to him: 'I hope you don't mind cats?' Whereupon Noel advanced, and seized 'One' in an embrace which would have flattered any star. And then –

in that unique and clipped diction of his, which was still crystalline, even though it came through a veil of fur, he said: 'My dear Beverley, I adore all animals with such an unreasoning passion that I cannot see a WATER BISON without BURSTING into tears.'

But all this is keeping us from 'Five', who is waiting outside the door.

§ 11

'Why did you have to have "Five" at all?' you may ask. 'Surely "One" and "Four" were enough?'

The reason was really psychological. My cats are served, as all cats should be served, by a doctor, a dentist, a coiffeur, a manicurist and a psychiatrist. (They have no need of a ballet master, because there is nothing that such a person could teach them, though they could certainly give a few tips to *him*). These five attendants are all contained in the person of a charming veterinary surgeon whose name, for reasons of professional etiquette, I must not mention. She gives them occasional pills, examines their teeth and nails, sees that coats are glossy and – most important of all – inquires into the state of their souls.

One day she was stroking 'One' on the kitchen table, and looking deep into his eyes.

'How old is "One"?' she asked.

' "One" is six. And "Four" is five.'

'It sounds like some frightful conundrum,' she said. 'But it all adds up to middle age.'

I felt rather indignant at this. 'Really! Neither of them has a sign of a tummy. They leap about all day like mad and there isn't a tree in the garden they don't climb.'

'All of which,' she observed, 'might equally apply to yourself.'

'Thank you.'

'The fact remains that if you were to translate their ages into human terms, "One" is forty-two and "Four" is thirty-five. Which is getting on.'

'It is indeed,' I agreed, gloomily. 'What ought we to do about it?'

'I suggest that they want freshening up. Young companionship. New ideas. In fact . . . another kitten. And I think I know just the one to suit them.'

This was a completely revolutionary idea, opening up almost illimitable vistas of delight, but also of danger. It would initiate an entirely new era in my life. It would require the most detailed and painful consideration from every point of view, and I felt it was somewhat inconsiderate of Miss X—— to have proposed it so suddenly, without giving me time to prepare for the shock.

However, if it had to be, it had to be, and one must go into training for it. The season was, fortunately, propitious; it was the beginning of May, which would mean that the new kitten – who was automatically baptized 'Five' – would be able to embark at once upon an outdoor life, without incurring any grave risks of chill. Not, Miss X—— assured me, that he was likely to be delicate; he was a farm kitten, who was used to sleeping in the stables, and eating anything that came his way.

'What does he look like?' I asked her.

'He is black and grey with a very bushy tail. He has a white chest with a grey shirt-front. And a white face with a big black blob across it, which makes him look as though he had put his nose in a soot-bag.'

This was, it will be generally agreed, a most rapturous description. I could hardly contain myself.

The first thing to do, of course, was to cancel all appointments, in order to have a free hand to deal with the various crises which a new kitten brings in its train. 'Five' was due to arrive on Sunday, May 10th, so it would be necessary to be completely disengaged until at least the seventeenth. This meant a good deal of telephoning, which in some cases led to acrimonious exchanges.

'But you *can't* chuck. We've got *seats*. Five? Five what? Oh – I *see*. How amusing. But what has that got to do with it? Happen to him? *What* might happen to him? Really, it's too ridiculous. Isn't Gaskin there? Well . . . why can't he cope? Two of you to deal with him? What *are* you talking about? You sound as though you were importing an entire menagerie. I've never heard anything so ridiculous and Angela will never speak to you again.'

Such social embarrassments are inevitable in the lives of cat-lovers. They do not worry us overmuch; they are a small price to pay for the enjoyment of feline companionship.

The great day came. The decks of Merry Hall, so to speak, were stripped for action. 'One' and 'Four' were shut up in the music-room, looking highly suspicious. A special plate of fish was set aside. The Box was placed in a tactful but accessible position in the scullery. If I state that The Box was filled with a layer of silver sand it will be unnecessary to describe its purpose in greater detail.

At last he arrived. We opened the basket in the hall. As the lid was gently lifted an enchanting vision was disclosed. The shirt-front was there, just as Miss X—— had promised. And the bushy tail, and the blob on the nose, which looked even more like a patch of soot than I had dared to hope. To crown it all, there was a pair of the largest green eyes you have ever seen.

Those eyes blinked, and regarded us with a mild interest. Apparently we would pass – for the moment, at any rate. Then they turned away and looked towards the window. A large bluebottle was buzzing against the pane. 'Five' stared at it with great concentration. Then he crouched, and swayed, and with a sudden leap he sprang out of the basket on to the window-ledge. He missed the bluebottle, but it did not matter. The ice was broken; his career at Merry Hall had begun.

§ III

There were sterner ordeals ahead, however, than bluebottles. 'One' and 'Four' had yet to be encountered, and this was likely to be so nerve-wracking a business that we put it off until he had eaten some fish, lapped some milk, and availed himself of the amenities of The Box . . . which, I was thankful to observe, he used with precision and *aplomb*.

At last it could be delayed no longer. I took 'Five' in my arms, and walked to the door of the music-room. Gaskin, it had been arranged, was to wait outside, and only to enter in case there were sounds of violent conflict or cries for help.

I opened the door and went in.

'One' was sitting bolt upright on the piano, as still as a statue, except for an occasional sharp lashing of the tail, staring straight ahead of him. 'Four' was sitting on the window-ledge, with his back to the window – a most unnatural position for him, since he is an inveterate window-gazer. He too was staring straight ahead.

I took a step forward. 'Five's' small head swivelled rapidly round, looking in amazement at this vast new universe. I saw the blue of the chandelier reflected in the green of his eyes. He was still quite relaxed, but breathing rather quickly.

I took another step forward.

' "One",' I whispered. ' "One." Look who I've brought to see you!'

For a moment 'One' did not see 'Five'. He only heard my voice, rose up, and prepared to jump down to greet me. Then, he noticed the little bundle in my arms. He paused in his tracks, as though frozen; the fur rose on his back, the thin dark tail slowly swelled into a fox's bush, and from the depths of his throat came that most awful and poignant of sounds – the wail of the Siamese cat.

It cannot be translated into words, this primitive lament, and I fancy that it would be difficult to translate into music. It might be attempted by an exceptionally accomplished performer with a *cor anglais*, or even a muted saxophone. If I were scoring it for orchestra I should probably combine the *cor anglais* and the saxophone, on an ascending passage, with flutes in descending thirds, in order to convey the strange combination of ferocity and despair. One might also bring in a harp in the background, though I am not so sure of this. Very few modern composers could be trusted with so important a theme, though Tschaikowski might have made a fair job of it. For of all the sounds betwixt heaven and hell, the wail of the Siamese cat strikes the clearest tone of naked grief.

'Oh, "One",' I said. 'Please! Do not be foolish, "One". Look!'

I went a little nearer, and again showed him 'Five', who – I must say – was behaving with remarkable *sang-froid*.

Then, before I knew what was happening, 'Five' had leapt from my arms, taken six straight steps up to 'One', paused, and tapped him sharply on the nose.

Such bravado, as far as I am aware, has no parallel in history, ancient or modern. Ajax and the lightning, David and Goliath, Drake and the Armada, Oliver Twist and the beadle . . . these legends pale before that act of 'Five's'.

Never in the whole of his conquering career had any living creature, human or animal, dared to cross 'One', or even to suggest, by word or deed, that he was not the monarch of all he surveyed. What – oh what – was going to happen?

What happened was so swift that it is difficult to describe. There was a last blood-curdling wail, an acrobatic leap in the air, and 'One' shot past me, through the open door, to vanish in the shadows of the copper beech. A moment later 'Four' followed in his tracks.

The 'psychological treatment' prescribed by Miss X——

had evidently got off to a flying start. My own fear was lest it should prove too drastic. Time alone would show. Meanwhile 'Five' remained master of the field.

§ I V

Of all the delightful ceremonies attendant upon the arrival of a new kitten in the house, perhaps the most exciting of all is the first introduction to the garden. This usually comes on the third or fourth day. By then the kitten can be assumed to have found its way about the house; it will no longer rush under the sofa when it hears the piano, nor be transfixed with horror when it sees you in the bath. ('Five', apart from his initial gesture of independence, showed all these normal reactions.) By then, too, it will have grown almost as tired of The Box as you are yourself.

So into the garden you go.

You step out of doors. The fresh wind blows in your face. The little body grows tense, and there is a tremendous amount of head-swivelling. Swivel to the left, for the wind is sweeping through the branches of the weeping willow. Swivel to the right, for the cellar door is swinging on its hinges. Sharp swivel upwards, for a swallow has darted across the sky. Tenser and tenser grows the little body . . . there is a sudden, contorted scramble of panic . . . and you retire swiftly to the doorway, and set the kitten down once more in the great safety of Indoors.

'It's all right,' you say to it. 'It's quite all right. It isn't death and destruction and danger. It's just a garden, and it's waiting to welcome you. But I do understand how you feel.'

And indeed I do. At least, I try to do. We are such clumsy clods, in our dealings with the animals, that we can never be quite sure. When you think that this furry creature has only been in the world for eight weeks, and when you remember that it is an acutely sensitive bundle of instincts and reactions, it is an almost terrifying responsibility to introduce it to the world for the first time. How can we tell what messages of alarm or delight are being transmitted through that cold pink nose? How can we visualize the fantastic pictures that must be flashing across the pale green screen of those startled eyes? The willow tree may be a monster, the swinging door a dragon, the sweeping swallow a messenger from heaven or from hell. I suppose we all play at being God, sometimes. Well, if I were God I would try to arrange that for a brief period in the life of every man and every woman, he or she should be given the soul and shape of an animal, that we should see the world, if even for a moment, through the eyes of a kitten or a puppy or a squirrel or a seagull. Perhaps, one day in the long corridors of time, it may be our fate to do so. I rather hope it will.

CHAPTER TWELVE

AN OLD MAN'S FANCY

IT was in my fourth year at Merry Hall that Oldfield suddenly threw us all into alarm and despondency by announcing that he was not going to pay his annual visit to the Chelsea Flower Show.

I shall never forget the occasion. It was a warm day in the middle of May, and Gaskin told me the news just after dinner.

'But that's out of the question,' I exclaimed. 'He's always gone. He and Mrs. Oldfield. They look forward to it all through the year.'

'He says he's got too much to do.'

'Surely he can take *one* day off?'

'He says no.'

'But if I got the odd man to come an extra day a week . . . two extra days?'

'He says it still wouldn't make any difference.'

I finished my dinner in a mood of some despondency. If Oldfield did not go to the Flower Show I had a suspicion that I should never hear the last of it. It had been his custom to go up early on the morning of the third day, returning at about nine o'clock; and he usually hovered around on the lawn, in his black Sunday suit, before going to bed, in order to catch me and exchange notes. One year it was the vegetable display of the Farmers Union that caught his fancy, another year he would dilate on the rival claims of the principal seedsmen. And always he connected the glories of the present with the glories of the past, attaching to some particular flower the characteristics of one of his past employers. Thus, concerning calceolarias and the late Mr. and Mrs. Dove, for whom he had worked before the days of Mr. Stebbing. . . .

'They was the most beautiful calceolaries I ever did see, today . . . twice the size of when I grew 'em, and all sorts of shades they never had before. Now Doovz couldn't abide calceolarias. At least, they *could* abide 'em in the beginning, but Mrs. Doove, she began to get ideas when Mr. Doove made his money. And one day she read in t'paper that calceolarias weren't smart no more, and nobody liked 'em in society. That was in 1910, that was. And Mrs. Doove was all for society. So she come to me and say "Oldfield, chuck 'em away, the whole God's collection of 'em." So I asks her why. And she says nobody likes calceolarias no more. So I says to her as I liked 'em. "That may be," she said, "but the best people don't like 'em." So I says to her, "What you mean is they're not *oop* enough for you." '

That picture has a nostalgic appeal – the determined Edwardian lady in her trailing dress and her floppy hat, grinding the stick of her parasol into the gravel – confronting Oldfield over forty years ago in my own garden, and telling him to chuck away the calceolarias. He must have loved them very much to have dared, in those days, to make the suggestion that they weren't 'oop enough' for her.

If Oldfield did not go to the Flower Show I should hear no more stories like that. I decided to do my best to persuade him.

§ I I

It was nearly nine o'clock when I went out to the kitchen garden. Oldfield was not about. Maybe, for once in a way, he had turned in early . . . if you can call stopping work at nine o'clock turning in early.

It was several weeks since I had been able to take a close stock of what he had been doing, but it needed only the most cursory glance to realize that he had been doing far too much.

In the frames, which lay open to the evening sunlight, there were enough ivy geraniums, pink and scarlet, to fill a large bed. I had told him that I only wanted about a dozen to fill the two urns on the front wall.

There were at least thirty superbly grown fuchsias, of the common bedding variety, and a dozen giant pink fuchsias in pots, each beautifully staked and delicately tied with bass. These were the progeny of two which I had admired a couple of years before.

There were six closely packed boxes of stocks and asters, and vast quantities of gaillardias – a flower for which I have no great enthusiasm. There were serried ranks of dahlias, verbenas and chrysanthemums, a vast display of zinnias, some fifty Bermuda lilies, and rows and rows of all sorts of uncommon things of which I had rashly given him seeds, at one time or another, such as the electric blue Morning Glory, which I had bought from a shop just outside the Gare du Nord. We now had enough of them to cover the whole house.

And this was only the bare beginning. The greenhouses were both packed to the roof, and all round them were ranged masses of vegetables, such as dwarf French beans and special yellow tomatoes, and early celery, all superbly grown in pots, waiting to be planted out. If you looked beyond them, to the kitchen garden, you saw row upon row of peas – six crops of them, and sweet peas as well, and so many rows of broad beans, onions, carrots, spinach and the like, that it was impossible to imagine how we should manage to eat a quarter of them. All this in addition to the asparagus beds, the raspberry beds, the currant beds, the lily beds, the beds of tulips, roses, irises, and lilies-of-the-valley, the peaches on the wall, the espalier pears, etc. etc. It made me tired even to look at them.

You may tell me that it was ungrateful to complain of such largesse. But one is human; one differs, in several quite marked respects, from an Oriental slave-driver; and I could not forget that a garden such as this would tax the energies of two young men of twenty-five, whereas Oldfield was one old man rising seventy-six.

Something must be done. Even as I was asking myself what that something would be, there was a step behind me. Oldfield had come back to work – at a quarter past nine.

§ I I I

'Good evening, Oldfield.'
'Evening, sir.'
'It's warm tonight.'
A faint snort was the only response. He walked straight past me to pick up the watering cans. This was a bad sign. When Oldfield shows no desire to comment on the weather it means that a storm is brewing inside him. Oldfield and the weather are ancient enemies. If you say that it looks like rain he will tell you that it will 'hold off'. If you feel that warmer days are ahead, he sniffs and smells a frost. His prophecies are usually reinforced by the opinions of a person whom he calls 'man on t'wireless'. I suspect that this gentleman is largely mythical, for he is quoted on every conceivable occasion to give point to Oldfield's personal opinions. For instance, if you suggest that it is a good thing to cut off the dead heads of the

lilacs, up pops 'man on t'wireless' to proclaim that it makes no difference at all. If you praise the virtues of nicotine dust against red spider, 'man on t'wireless' laughs it to scorn. I think I shall invent my own 'man on t'wireless'. In all forms of controversy he is the ideal *deus ex machina*.

Where were we? Oh yes . . . I had just said 'It's warm tonight'. And Oldfield had not replied, but had walked away to pick up his watering cans.

'What's this I hear about you're not going to the Flower Show?'

He still made no reply, but walked past me again, back to the big tank under the fig tree. Into this he dipped his cans.

No cold tap water for Oldfield. It must have stood all day, warming in the sun.

'Aren't you going?' I repeated.

'Nay. I'm not going.' He put down his cans and folded his arms. ''Twill be the first time in forty years.'

'Won't that be rather a pity?'

'Aye, 'twill be a pity.' He picked up his cans again, and went over to the frames, to water the seed-boxes.

There I followed him. 'Surely you can take one day off?'

The absurdity of the suggestion made him snort. He did not even turn round.

'If I got the odd man in for an extra day? Or perhaps for two extra days?'

'There's no amount of odd men could cope with it.'

'But Oldfield, we never used to get in such a fix in the old days.'

'T'old days?' He turned round and glared at me. 'You've been oop to things, since t'old days!'

This, I felt, was really somewhat unfair. It was he, not I, that had been oop to things. It was not my fault that we had a small farm of fuchsias and enough geraniums to plant the gardens outside Buckingham Palace. However, it was useless to argue with him in his present mood, so I told him, shortly, that the odd man would be engaged, and that I hoped he would go to the Flower Show in spite of everything. And I bade him good night.

Well, he did go to the Flower Show, of course. And he did come to talk to me about it when he got back, in his black suit, and the 'man on t'wireless' was particularly vocal in flatly contradicting every opinion I ventured.

But the situation remained tense. In spite of all my efforts, and those of the odd man, the garden seemed to grow larger and larger. And as it grew, Oldfield worked harder and harder.

'What are we to *do*?' I asked Gaskin.

'You should be firm,' said Gaskin. 'You should give him a definite order. You should say that a third of the kitchen garden has got to be left to go wild, and that would be the end of it.'

'You know perfectly well, Gaskin, that there would *not* be end of it. I told him two years ago that a third of the kitchen garden had got to be left to go wild, and what happened? Nothing. He dug it and double-dug it till he nearly dropped, and then he got me to order a mass of manure, and we had the most marvellous crop of peas and broad beans we've ever had.'

'Then you should tell him to shut up one of the greenhouses. It's ridiculous to have two greenhouses as well as the conservatory.'

'I know quite well that it is. And I did tell him to shut up one of the greenhouses. He didn't take the least notice, and six weeks later he made me agree to having Mr. Young repair them both, and that cost me eighty pounds.'

'You're too weak. That's what it is. If I had *my* way . . .'

'Well? What would you do?'

For once in a while, Gaskin was at a loss. In his heart of hearts, he knew that there wasn't anything that anybody could do. Oldfield would work till he dropped. And probably, if one tried to stop him, he would drop the sooner.

§ I V

Meanwhile, as the year progressed, and as this little floral drama reached the mild climax to which we are leading, I tried a number of innovations which might, I felt, mark the beginning of a less arduous era.

I began with very small things. One of them was an old cactus. It was among the many remnants that I had inherited from Mr. Stebbing, and I chose it because Oldfield had once told me that Mrs. Oldfield hated it and wanted him to throw it away. It was, indeed, a hideous object, with diseased and spotted stems, like the flappers of a decrepit seal. For at least three hundred and sixty days out of the three hundred and sixty-five it remained dormant; but towards the end of every May it used to spring to life, and burst into a bonfire of scarlet blossom.

So one day I said to Oldfield, 'I think we might get rid of this, don't you?'

He paused. Then he said: ''Tis Mrs. Oldfield's.'

This was just what I had been waiting for. 'Yes,' I replied, brightly. 'I remember you telling me how much she disliked it.'

Another pause. ''Tis no trouble,' he said.

'Well, it has to be staked, and tied up, and kept out of draughts . . .' I did not continue the argument, but lifted the pot down, and put it near the door to remind him.

On the following day the cactus was still there.

'I thought we were going to put this on the rubbish heap?' I said.

'If we put it on t'rubbish heap, cats might sniff at it. And 'tis full of prickles.'

This was really the most blatant evasion. 'Then we shall have to bury it.'

'Seems a pity to bury it.'

I had a sudden idea. 'I think I know somebody in London who might like it,' I said. 'Next time I go up in the car I'll take it with me.'

A few days later I took it. As soon as I was at a safe distance from Meadowstream, motoring along a quiet road, I seized the cactus and threw it towards the ditch. It fell short, and broke into fragments on the road, where it almost certainly caused somebody a puncture. I did not stop to pick it up; I was too glad to be rid of it.

But one could not motor round the country hurling cactuses out of the window, and strewing the roadside with boxes of cuttings and pots of superfluous chrysanthemums. People would think one eccentric, and there might be inquiries by the police.

Meanwhile, the garden grew and grew, and whenever I tried to get rid of anything, Oldfield thwarted me. For instance, there were two old orange trees in the greenhouse which never produced anything except a few yellow leaves and an endless quantity of black fly. I moved them into the cold house and told Oldfield, quite firmly, that they were either to be thrown away or given to somebody. The orange trees duly disappeared and I congratulated myself on having won a small victory. A month later I saw 'One' sniffing at a pile of sacks under the staging. I knelt down to see what he was after. There, carefully hidden from my marauding eye, were the orange trees, freshly watered and freshly sprayed. They are with us to this day.

Then one day I had an idea. It came to me with the first chill breath of the North-East wind. If only it were not for the warm greenhouse, I thought, where so many plots were hatched all through the winter, so many extra boxes of seedlings brought on, so many superfluous cuttings grown to maturity . . . if only it were not for this tempting haven, Old-field would be *forced* to reduce, and the whole of the rest of the year would be far simpler. Needless to say, I had no intention of shutting off the heat altogether, there must always be just enough to keep out the frost, for the sake of the bougainvillaeas and the mimosas. But in future he would be allowed only a minimum of fuel, and if he did not like it he would have to lump it.

It was an ideal winter for making such a decision. The annual coal crisis was worse than ever; householders had been warned to economize; and when I suggested to Gaskin that it was high time we put on the central heating he replied that we could not start it before November, and that even then we should have to go very slow indeed.

'And every day,' he added indignantly, 'that old man comes along and asks me when he's going to get another load for his greenhouse! I told him that if there ever *is* another load, it'll go straight into the cellar. My kitchen's like an ice-house. You should talk to him . . . you really should.'

It is at moments like these that I am inclined to regret the absence of a wife. 'Talking to people' is a wife's privilege. I learned that, as a small boy, by observing the conduct of my elders and betters. If there was trouble with a cook or a house-maid, as there usually was, my father would airily say to my mother, 'You should talk to her,' and dismiss the subject. If matters came to a head with the boot-boy . . . 'You should talk to him; *I* wouldn't stand it.' My mother's obvious retort was that he didn't have to stand it; all the unpleasantness fell on her shoulders. But wives did not speak like that in those days; they resigned themselves to their fate; and I imagine that they still do. It is always the woman who has to go out to the back premises, trembling with nerves and longing to sink through the floor, in order to confront some angry creature, who folds her arms, and tosses her head, and makes her wish that *she* had been born into one of the privileged professions, such as domestic service.

Oldfield never treated me like that. Oldfield was a gentle-man. He employed subtler methods. When I went out to 'talk to him' about the fuel situation he merely sighed, and referred to his chrysanthemums.

'Never did I see 'em so backward,' he said. 'I doubt if they'll be in bloom by Christmas, at this rate.'

If you had been with us you might have thought that he was exaggerating. The shelves were packed with a magnificent collection of chrysanthemums, already three feet high, with buds beginning to form. They were all expertly staked, tied, and disbudded, and there was not a speck of disease on any of them. In six weeks time, they would be a carnival of gold and bronze and white and rose, unless I was very much mistaken. Or unless I cut down the heat.

I *must* be firm.

'Well, Oldfield,' I said. 'We can't help it. We'll have to make do.'

'Aye,' he retorted. 'That's all it is, in these days. Making do. If Mr. Stebbing was alive. . . .'

But I was in too emotional a condition to listen to what Mr. Stebbing might or might not have done if he had been alive. The chrysanthemums were pleading with me; Oldfield was reproaching me – merely because I was trying to be practical and to save people trouble. It was all most unfair and most exhausting. I suddenly found myself longing to have a skin like an ox, ten thousand a year free of tax, and a pent-house in New York, with nothing to worry about except a cactus and a few pots of ivy.

'Anyway,' I said shortly, 'I'm afraid we've no alternative. There's no more fuel to be had. If there are sharp frosts . . . well, that's just too bad.'

With which I beat an ungraceful retreat, leaving a sharp frost – a very sharp frost – behind me, in the shape of an old gentleman entirely surrounded by chrysanthemums.

§ v

The climax came one bitter afternoon in November, when I returned from a visit to London. The metropolis had seemed even more squalid than usual, the streets dirtier, the crowds ruder, the shops drabber, and the food more universally repulsive. I could not wait to get back to the warm music-room, and a blazing log fire. There would be time to pick a nice bunch of border chrysanthemums before tea, and then there would be a couple of hours for the Second Scherzo – the waterfall passages were almost frozen through lack of practice. After which there would be an omelette, and some of Oldfield's marvellous celery, which I should make even more celerified by dipping it into celery salt. Then there would be more logs on the fire, and the cats would be brought in, and if the telephone rang I should be out to everybody but Winston Churchill – from whom I was not expecting any immediate attentions – and life was altogether delectable.

But when I opened the front door, something was wrong. A chill pervaded the house. Merry Hall, in winter, is one of the few English homes which, in my opinion, are adequately heated. In other words, it is apt to asphyxiate everybody but Americans, who feel deliriously at home in it. But today, it was as cold as a poverty-stricken parsonage on the Yorkshire moors.

I walked over to the radiator and put my hand on it. It was barely luke-warm. Something must be done, and done quickly. Which meant, of course, that Gaskin must be mobilized.

'What on earth has happened to the central heating?' I demanded.

'You may *well* ask' retorted Gaskin. 'It's that old man. He just won't put it on properly. If I've spoken to him once today I've spoken to him a dozen times.'

'But what's the idea?'

'He wants the coke for his greenhouse. What's more, he's been taking it out of the cellar. For all he cares we can freeze to death. Just look!' He drew me to the window and pointed to the cellar door. 'He's been barrowing it up and wheeling it across the lawn for the past two hours. What's more, I believe . . . yes . . . he *has* lit the greenhouse fire!'

Sure enough, in the distance, through the branches of the copper beech, I could see a thin thread of blue smoke ascending.

'This is intolerable', I said.

'It certainly is,' agreed Gaskin. ' "One" and "Four" have been sitting so close to the logs in the music-room ever since breakfast that "One" hasn't got a whisker left on one side of his face. And he still isn't warm.'

'I suppose you couldn't . . .' A look in Gaskin's eye prevented me from finishing the sentence. 'No. I'll have to go and speak to him myself.'

'You certainly will.'

'After all, I did tell him quite definitely that the fire was not to be lit till December 1st.'

'You did. What's more, I reminded him of it. But it's no use me saying anything. He just grunts.'

Gaskin helped me into my overcoat and I went outside. This was a very distressful business. As I crossed the lawn I could not help thinking how very much nicer it must be to be the employed rather than the employer. The employer always has the wrong end of the stick; it is always he who has to be disagreeable, to make scenes and fusses – and incidentally, to pay for doing so. I had very little notion of what I was going to say to Oldfield, nor how I should phrase it. I could not march in and say 'Put that fire out.' Such a course was unthinkable. I had a humiliating suspicion that whatever I said would begin with the phrase . . . 'Don't you think, Oldfield, that it might possibly be a good idea if perhaps . . .' I have gone through life asking people if they do not think that it might possibly be a good idea if perhaps. Bitter experience has taught me that people, when thus addressed, seldom do.

Outside the greenhouse I hovered, trying to summon up courage. Oldfield had turned the lights on, and was standing inside, with his back to me. I could not help admitting that it all looked very warm and cosy, the blue smoke rising to the grey sky, the mist creeping over the glass-panes, and the light sparkling on the snowy buds of the chrysanthemums, which were just on the point of opening. In fact, when I remembered the chill of the house, it looked a great deal *too* cosy. I realized that I was shivering, and this made me indignant. I would delay no longer. I stepped forward to go inside.

Then I paused. What was the matter with Oldfield? He had not moved since I had been standing there: his head had sunk on to his chest. Was it my fancy, or was he groping for support? Good heavens – this was terrible. There must be something wrong for him to act like that. I ran down the steps and opened the door.

'Oldfield, are you all right?'

He was leaning against the staging, with his eyes half closed. I had a sudden dread that he was about to collapse. All that I had intended to say to him went out of my mind, indeed, the whole purpose of my visit was forgotten.

I went over to him. 'Are you all right?'

'I come over giddy, like.' His voice was very faint.

'You'd better sit down for a minute.' I cleared some pots off the little brick well. 'There. That's better.' He sat down heavily. 'Would you like me to get you something? A drop of whisky?'

He shook his head. 'No sir. Thank you kindly.'

I waited in silence. He seemed to be breathing normally, but I didn't like the look of things.

''Tisn't often that I come over giddy, like,' he murmured.

'Just sit still, and don't bother to talk.'

'T'last time I come over giddy like, 'twas in time of Doovz.'

'Yes. You must tell me about it some time, but just for the moment . . .'

'That was nigh on thirty years ago,' he continued, ignoring me. 'Almost to a day.' He drew a deep sigh.

'Rest quietly for a little while,' I pleaded.

'I know 'twas almost to a day,' he went on, 'because t'chrysanthemums was just as they are now, with t'blooms on point of opening. Just when you have to be on t'look-out for a sharp frost.'

For the first time he raised his head, and looked me full in the face, with a look of infinite reproach in his one good eye. He made me feel an utter brute, and I wished, all the more, that he would stop talking. But his voice seemed to be gathering strength, with rather surprising speed, so I let him go on.

'Aye,' he repeated, looking round him at the serried ranks of magnificent blooms, 'just when you have to be on t'look-out.' He allowed his hand to rest for a moment on one of the pipes, which was pleasantly warm. He gave a grunt, and nodded.

This was terrible. Here was my faithful old gardener, at the end of his days, about to expire in the greenhouse, and I seemed to have been forced into a position where I was callously denying him a few lumps of coke to comfort him and his flowers. I have never felt so acutely uncomfortable.

'Yes, Oldfield,' I began, intending to tell him that somehow or other we would contrive some fuel . . . when he again interrupted me.

''Twas a Sunday afternoon,' he observed, 'and I'd gone for a walk up Leith Hill. Thirty years ago I was a rare 'un for walking. I'd gone up hill to have a look at t'spindles. You never saw such spindles in all your life. Never. I must have stayed too long looking at 'em, for it come on dark, and just as it come on dark, I come over giddy.'

'So what did you do?'

'What did I do? I sit down in t'hedge, and I get out a piece of paper, and I writes down my name and address.'

AN OLD MAN'S FANCY

'That was very wise of you.'

'I writes "To Whom It May Concern", like they put on t'placards. Then I writes, will they please go straight home and stoke up fires for chrysanthemums.'

I turned away, for I found myself suddenly afflicted by a mist over the eyes.

'Aye,' he said. 'I reckoned they could leave me in t'hedge for a while, and I'd be all right. But I was worried about my fires. There was a frost coming on.'

He rose slowly to his feet.

I turned round again. 'I wouldn't get up yet, Oldfield.'

He gripped the staging. His one eye seemed to bore through me.

'There's a frost coming on tonight,' he said.

I nodded.

'Looks like being a sharp 'un.'

He waved his hand, in a gesture of awkward dignity, towards the chrysanthemums, as though he were pleading for them. Then he said "Tis a long way to wheel coke from cellar across t'lawn. And if I was to come on giddy again. . . .'

He paused, still fixing me with his one eye. He was waiting for what I should say, as though it were a sentence of life or death. I had the fancy that the flowers were waiting, too, and for the same reason. It was a crucial moment in our relationship, there in the warm greenhouse, with the white buds glowing in the shadows, and the chill of the November mists creeping up against the glass.

Well, I know what I *ought* to have said. I ought to have said 'Oldfield, you are an old scoundrel. You know quite well that the times are out of joint, that fuel is impossible to get, that all sorts of people far richer and more important than ourselves are being forced to cut things down and let things go. But you will not cut a thing down and you will not let a thing go. And I ought to give you a severe ticking off.'

But the hell of it was that I loved him for it. I loved the

courage, and the doggedness, and the sublime refusal to face facts. I even loved the art – how else could one describe it? – with which he had staged this scene and told me this story.

For, between you and me, I do not believe that Oldfield had 'come over giddy' at all.

One thing, at least, is certain. He has never 'come over giddy' since.

CHAPTER THIRTEEN

THE GHOST

I BELIEVE in ghosts, but do not go in search of them. If any wandering spirit should chance to have need of me, and endeavour to manifest itself, I trust that I should treat it with courtesy. But I should prefer that it had gone next door.

All the same, we were quite prepared for Merry Hall to have a ghost; indeed, it would have been faintly disappointing if there had been no signs of one. After all, the house was built in the year 1788, which was an excellent year for ghosts. The French Revolution was about to break, and before the roses had climbed more than a few feet up the new brick walls there would be many strange figures in the lanes and the highways roundabout, living ghosts, fleeing from the Terror. In the village inn there would have been talk of Boney and his legions, and the same brick walls would have glowed to the flare of beacons on the distant hills.

Yes, there might be many ghosts at Merry Hall – Georgian ghosts, Regency ghosts, early Victorian ghosts – apart from the distinctly twentieth-century ghost of Mr. Stebbing, whom we have already encountered. Apart from this latter, I had a feeling that if there *were* any ghosts, they would be nice cosy ghosts, with a sense of the proprieties. They would not lurk in corners, with sinister expressions, nor tap rudely on the windows; they would betray themselves only by a graceful shadow, now and then, on the staircase, and they would leave behind them a scent of lavender. There would be no bangings nor clatterings – only an occasional sigh behind a closed door, or, in the far distance, the tinkling of a spinet.

Such were the ghosts that I had envisaged. The reality proved to be very different.

This is a difficult story to tell, for since it is in all essentials a true story – else there would be no point in it – there can be no building up of 'atmosphere', no artful hints and dodges; we must be strictly factual. And the first fact that greets us, oddly enough, is that in the year 1895 a horse called Ilex, owned by a certain Mr. J. C. Masterman, won the Grand National. And that this horse was bred at Merry Hall.

If you think that this is just another piece of whimsey you can look it up in the reference books. I did myself.

Those were the bare facts. As time went on, they began to be clothed with a few more details. Some of these were supplied by an old man whom we will call C——. He arrived to do odd jobs in the garden, and he was so quick, and seemed to find his way about so well, that one day I asked him if he had known the garden in the past. 'Known this garden?' he chuckled. 'Aye – I should say I'd known 'im!' And he told me that he had worked here as a boy, nearly sixty years ago, in the days of Mr. Masterman himself.

From him I learned that Masterman had a passion for his horses that passed the bounds of reason. There were six of them in all. I will not attempt to describe them, for I know nothing about horses. The horses I like best are the sort that drape themselves against country gates, demanding sugar.

They are large, clumsy, amiable, and usually – poor things – greatly bothered by flies. These, to me, are real horses. I cannot raise much enthusiasm for the other sort, the sleek, sharp, swift sort, that one sees in the paintings of Sir Alfred Munnings. I am sure that they are very nice, and I am glad that people put blankets over them, but we have nothing to say to one another.

These six horses, then, used to caper up and down the lawns of Merry Hall, under the doting eye of Mr. Masterman. He used to visit them at all hours of the day and night, patting them, fondling them, talking to them for hours on end. He had an old groom called Withers, a little man who looked like a fox, and sometimes he would go out to the stables with a bottle of champagne, and tell Withers to open it, and they would sit there, in the smell of the straw and the dung, toasting the horses till the moon was high.

Then came the Grand National, which was won by Ilex. Whether this was too much of an emotional strain for Mr. Masterman, or whether there had been an excessive consumption of champagne, we shall never know, but shortly afterwards he took to his bed. In a few weeks he died.

As he was dying, they propped him up in the window – the same window from which I look out, every morning, on to the copper beech – and Withers led the horses over the lawn for him to see. Up and down, backwards and forwards – the little foxy groom, followed by the stable lads, in a mournful cavalcade. Then a hand was waved, and a blind was drawn, and Withers led the horses back to the stables for the last time.

§ 11

That is the background of our story.

We now take you over to Miss Mint, as they say on the wireless.

On a certain Sunday night in late October – a few days after the end of summer-time, when darkness falls at half past five – Miss Mint was coming to supper. The idea was that we should watch the television play, and I was going to fetch her in the car. But on the night before, the car broke down, so I telephoned to say that I would hire one in the village.

'Nonsense,' she replied. 'All that expense! I shall come by bus.'

'But it only goes to the village.'

'I shall walk through the lanes.'

She was a determined little thing, in spite of all her timidity, and to my protests she merely replied that if she did not come by bus, she would not come at all. Two pounds at the very least, a car would cost, and if that was not sheer wickedness she would like to know what was. Rain? There was no chance of it. It was a lovely October day; there might be a hint of frost when the sun went down, but that did not matter. And the moon would be nearly full.

So we left it at that.

I prowled round, getting things ready. There were always special things to be done, when Miss Mint was coming. For instance, there had to be a number of Lilliputian bunches of mixed flowers, placed in strategic positions, on tables and mantelpieces. These were arranged in such containers as silver salt-cellars, liqueur glasses, egg-cups, and even match-boxes, lined with tin and painted white. Whether Miss Mint enjoyed looking at them as much as I enjoyed making them will always be a moot question. They were certainly among the major pleasures of my life. One could make enchanting arrangements out of a late rosebud, the tender tip of a montbretia, some baby leaves of rose geranium, and any of the tiny wild flowers that might still be sheltering in the hedges.

After the bunches had all been inspected and 'topped up' – I always put in the water with a fountain-pen filler – the cocktail tray had to be prepared. Miss Mint's cocktail was a major ceremony. No, she would not dream of having one. Just a salted almond. That would be delicious. Well – perhaps a very small glass of Italian vermouth, just to keep me company, though she was sure it would 'go to her head'. But what else was I putting in it? Oh really – it was very wicked of me, she would be quite incapable. Whereupon, with sparrow-like sips and a great many exclamations of imminent intoxication – she would absorb, during the next ten minutes, a tiny glass of vermouth and ice-water, to which I had added a dewdrop of gin. This was Miss Mint's nearest approach to an orgy; it produced in both of us a feeling of extreme exhilaration and, indeed, of daring impropriety.

On this particular evening, Miss Mint was late. She should have been here by six o'clock and it was nearly half past. I began to reproach myself for allowing her to come by bus. True, it was only a short walk through the lanes, but the promise of a fine evening had not been fulfilled; the wind had risen, great clouds were piling up against the moon, and on the roof of the conservatory the first drops of rain were spattering. Perhaps I had better go down the lane and meet her half way? But no – Gaskin was out, we might miss each other, and there would be nobody to let her in. Better to wait.

Suddenly, through the rising wind, I heard a noise outside. It seemed to come from the front door. Not exactly a knocking, not quite a rapping, but rather a sort of dull sliding, as though someone were passing his hands over it, trying to effect a secret entry. I got up, stepped softly into the corridor, and listened. Yes, there it was again, this curious sliding sound, up and down, like hands groping in the darkness, against the woodwork.

But who could it be . . . or what? As I asked this question, my heart took a faster beat. For in the doorway there was a panel of clear glass, and if any human figure had been standing outside, I should have seen it. The moon was bright; a lozenge of silver shone clearly through the glass on to the faded carpet; but the pane of glass was otherwise a blank.

The door creaked in the rising wind, but it was no wind that caused this uncanny sound. A tap, a slide, a pause . . . a tap, a slide, a pause.

Well, one could not stand here doing nothing. For the space of some five seconds various precautionary measures flashed through my mind, such as the advisability of arming myself with a poker. But we only have one poker – a very pretty one of the time of Queen Anne – and though it is not madly good at poking I should have disliked to damage it. Even more would I have disliked to crack it on a living skull. There are men who enjoy cracking skulls and men who do not, and I am unashamedly on the side of the latter. Even the cracking of egg-shells has always seemed to me faintly Hunnish and Goth-like, and apt to be brutalizing in the long run.

So I took a deep breath, walked to the door, and flung it open.

There, half kneeling on the steps, was the figure of Miss Mint. She clutched at the door handle which had been wrenched from her hand.

'Forgive me,' she murmured. 'So foolish.'

Her hat fell off, and she fainted on to the floor.

§ I I I

And here is her story, which she told me an hour later, propped up on the sofa by the fire. She had made a swift recovery, and though she refused to allow a doctor to be called, she meekly accepted a sip of brandy, which brought a pretty flush to her cheeks. Then, with a rug over her knees, and 'One' purring on her lap, she seemed almost restored.

She began very simply, by explaining, without further ado,

that she had seen a ghost. Other women, less truthful and less direct, might have faltered and fluttered, and said that they thought they had seen a ghost, or that they might have seen a ghost. Miss Mint said that she *had* seen a ghost; and because she knew that she was telling the truth, it never occurred to one to doubt her.

'It was the very last thing I was expecting,' she went on, 'to see a ghost. I have never had any – inclinations – towards them. Nor they towards me. Besides, my mind was on other things, cheerful, everyday things. And then, it was so bright and pleasant in the bus, and I was able to sit in the front seat, which I always enjoy, as there were only a few other people inside. I think they were coming from Evensong.' She paused, and her fingers stopped stroking 'One'. 'How strange! I have only just thought of it. The lesson in this morning's service. Do you remember?'

'I'm afraid I missed this morning's service.'

'The witch of Endor! When "the woman with a familiar spirit" came to Saul, and summoned up the spirit of Samuel before him. And when Saul asked her . . . "What form is he of?" . . . she said, "An old man cometh up; and he is covered with a mantle".'

I nodded. 'Yes. I suppose that must be the first ghost story ever written in the world.'

'An old man . . . covered with a mantle,' repeated Miss Mint, as though to herself. Then she went on: 'But as I said before, I certainly wasn't thinking of ghosts when I left the bus at the inn, and started to walk down the lane.'

'What time was that?' I interrupted.

'Just before six.'

'But it was half past six when you got here, and it's an easy ten minutes walk. Had you been at the front door for very long?'

'No. Barely a minute. Oh dear . . . I'm afraid you'll think me very foolish, but that is part of the strangeness of it all.

The time element. Twenty minutes just disappeared. You see, when I lost my way. . . .'

'But how could you lose your way? There's no turning.'

'I know. Not today. But you see, I walked into the past.' She pressed her hands over her eyes for a moment. 'Let me think. It was when I noticed the great elms in the distance that I knew that something was happening – that time was playing a trick on me. If anybody had been with me, I think I would have turned back, or we might have said a little prayer together. I don't know. But by the time I had seen the elms it was too late; I was caught up in it all. For, of course, the elms were not there. You had them all cut down.

'And your garage was not there. There was a quite different building. I could not see it very clearly, because the elms hid most of it, and the clouds were coming over the moon. But even in the distance I saw that it was much bigger, and that it ran parallel with the road.

'I walked on; there was nothing else to do. I remember hearing the sound of my footsteps on the road; they were dragging, as though somebody was pulling me. And I remember thinking quite clearly . . . "I wonder what date this is? I wonder if I might meet somebody in a crinoline? It would be interesting to meet somebody in a crinoline." You see, my brain *was* working; I was not at all fuddled, and somehow I was not very frightened. Not yet.'

She paused. 'And then I saw the five-barred gate.'

'Was it on your right? Just in front of the old buildings?'

'Yes. How did you know?'

'I'll tell you later. Please go on.'

'A little old man was leaning over the gate. I could see him quite clearly, because the moon was out again. He was a funny little man, very short, with a foxy face. He was wearing breeches and leggings, and . . . and a sort of mackintosh cape.' She gave a nervous laugh. 'I nearly said "an old man, covered in a mantle". Of course, that was just a coincidence.'

'Of course.'

'He said "Good evening, ma'am". There was something about his voice that I did not like. Not that he was rude or . . . or . . . insolent or anything like that. Oh no! It just seemed that the voice came from a very long way away. From a far distance. It was like an echo. Oh dear, I really cannot explain myself.'

'You explain it very well.'

She managed the shadow of a smile. 'It is kind of you to say so. "Good evening, ma'am," he said. So I answered him with "Good evening," but before I could pass on he spoke again . . . from the same great distance, though his words were quite clear.'

'What did he say?'

'He leant forward over the top of the gate, and looked me straight in the face. "You'll be going to Merry Hall, ma'am?" he asked. "Yes," I said. He still kept staring at me. "It's a sad business, ma'am." I did not understand, but I suddenly felt very cold. "What has happened?" I asked. . . .'

She closed her eyes. For a moment I thought she was going to faint again, and put my hand on hers. She shook her head. 'I'm quite all right. I'm only trying to remember the exact words. Yes. Here they are. He said: "*It's a sad business, ma'am. He had the horses out early this morning for the last time. Walking past his window. And though he's been gone these twelve hours, and though he's lying there with the pennies on his eyes, he's still there at the window, looking out.*" '

There, to all intents and purposes, Miss Mint's story ends. What happened after that she does not know. All that we can say with certainty – and I do say it with certainty – is that for reasons which we shall never understand, she was chosen to walk into the past. And, equally mysteriously, to walk out again.

It only remains for me to add a postscript.

§ IV

I wanted Miss Mint to tell her story with the minimum of interruption, so I did not mention that at one point in it a distinct chill ran down my spine. This was when she mentioned the elms that had been cut down, the long, low building running parallel with the road, and the five-barred gate.

For in a drawer of the desk in the drawing-room, there lay an old map of Meadowstream, which had been lent to me by Mrs. Pattern, the vicar's wife, only the day before; and though I had only glanced at it, I remembered, very clearly, that the map had shown just such a building, in just such a place. And I knew that it had been demolished over fifty years ago.

When I had finally attended to Miss Mint, and gone up to wish her good night – (very small and sparrow-like she looked, in the huge bed with its patchwork quilt, and a pair of my pyjamas hanging round her shoulders like a shawl) – I went down to the drawing-room, closed the door behind me, and spread out the map on a table. It was dated 1895. It was a large map, printed on faded parchment, and the scale was 208 feet to the inch, which meant that Merry Hall and its out-buildings would occupy a space of about a square inch – quite large enough to show every detail clearly.

It took me some little time to find the house – I am very bad at maps – and for a few moments I almost forgot my errand, so fascinating was this glimpse into the past. Our Rose's cottage did not seem to be where it ought to have been at all; there was nothing but a triangular field, a small blue pond, and a large plantation in the background. The field was the right shape, and so was the blue pond, and the plantation must be the wood which stretched as far as Marius's house – yes, there it was, clearly marked – but there were no signs whatever of 'The Weathercocke'. This aroused the gloomiest suspicions about the authenticity of Rose's super-Tudor dwelling, and would obviously call for closer investigation in the future.

I traced my way over the parchment, down the winding lanes, past old chalk pits – so that was how Chalk Lane got its name – past numbers of wayside ponds, that had now been filled in, and at last I came to Merry Hall. Yes, there it was, as plain as a pikestaff, with a lot of little trees to mark the orchard, and the crescent wall, drawn into the lane, and the long L-shaped building, and . . .

And a small sign, like this , to mark the five-barred gate.

Which brings us to the final piece of evidence, and turns the spotlight on to 'One'.

I do not attach undue psychic importance to the reactions of animals; I do not think, for instance, that dogs invariably snarl at villains, and wag their tails at decent folk. They sometimes do precisely the reverse. I have a great friend whose large bulldog has a positive passion for burglars; it almost sits on the steps and invites them inside; not a word will it have said against them. On the other hand, it has such a noted aversion to the postman – a most estimable man with six children – that my friend is thinking of having her letters delivered Poste Restante.

It is the same with cats. Sometimes they know their friends, sometimes they don't. They will dig their claws into the best-intentioned fingers.

However, dogs and cats certainly 'see things'. There are some houses which no dog will pass without its tail between its legs. (One of them was the notorious Castle-a-Mare, on a hill overlooking Torbay.) And cats, especially at night, will suddenly jump up from their chairs, and bristle, and stare into space . . . at nothing. You can follow their eyes, and search as you will, there is nothing – just a blank wall, without even a fly on it. Yet there they stand, rigid, with dilated eyes, till the 'thing' has gone. It goes as quickly as it came, and the cat curls up again, licks itself, and falls asleep. There are doubtless a number of learned explanations of this phenomenon. The simplest seems to me also the best; the cat has seen a ghost.

Whatever it was that 'One' saw, on that particular evening – it was about a week before Miss Mint's adventure, and before I even knew of the existence of the map – it was enough to make him behave in the most peculiar way. We had been for one of our usual 'tours'. This had involved a visit to the orchard, to see the group of spindles, which were quite breath-taking in their beauty, and a perfect example of the way in which Nature can be vulgar and get away with it – for what could be more garish than a berry with a magenta shell and a brilliant orange pip? After the spindles there were the thorns, one of which had gone slightly mad, and produced quite the wrong sort of leaf below the graft. (Trees, I am sure, can lose their reason, just as much as human beings; I have several insane silver birches, to which I am greatly attached, and a half-witted *hamamelis mollis*, which always receives special attention.)

Then I had to lift 'One' up, because there were a number of rotting pears on the ground, and some wasps were still busy. So down we wandered again, over the big lawn and towards the outhouses, with 'One' very snug in the crook of my arm, staring up at me with his blue eyes, and squinting, as he always does when he is happy.

And suddenly, his eyes narrowed, he let out a piercing wail, and jumped out of my arms.

We were standing just at the top of the drive, looking towards the lane, with the garage on the left. This is a rough plan of the scene, with the present buildings in solid line, and the former buildings in dots:

'One' and I were standing at the point marked A. My intention was to walk down the drive to the point marked B, where there is a gap in a thick hedge of berberis, and to go through this gap to the fruit-room, to unload my pockets of a juicy collection of small sweet pears. 'One' knew the route perfectly well; we have taken it a hundred times; and he always liked jumping on to the shelves of the fruit-room to have a good sniff. But tonight he stayed there rigid, with his back arched, and that terrible wail coming from his throat, staring at the point where, in the old days, the five-barred gate had stood.

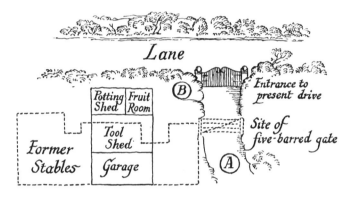

Well, I knew nothing about the existence of any ghostly gate, so I walked straight through it, towards B, and paused in the gap, calling for 'One' to follow. He did not move, but stayed there, wailing. 'There must be another cat in the bushes,' I thought . . . and yet 'One' was not looking towards the bushes, he was staring straight ahead. Perhaps it was something in the lane? I stepped outside, and peered up and down. There was nothing, nobody. The evening was very silent, and even the cawing of the rooks was hushed.

This was ridiculous. I could not stay here all night, indulging 'One's' fancies. So I called him in a different tone of voice – sharply, tersely – a voice to which he was not at all accustomed.

'One!' My nerves were on edge; otherwise I shouldn't have barked like that. Poor 'One', in spite of his wail of defiance, looked so helpless standing there in the twilight, such a frail small thing of beige fur and black fur and blue eyes. It was unkind and unintelligent to shout at him like that, when he was obviously distressed. I would go and pick him up, and take him indoors, and make a fuss of him.

I stepped forward. . . .

As I did so, 'One' suddenly crouched down, swaying to and fro, as cats always do when they are about to spring, and before I knew what was happening he had leapt high in the air, seeming to pause in full flight, and had landed again at my feet. And with a wild scramble he clambered up into my arms. His whole body was trembling as though he had a violent fever.

These are facts. You may not believe in my bougainvillaeas – (though I can produce photographic evidence of them) – and you may think that I have cast a parental glow of pride over my winter heathers – (though I can produce photographic evidence of them, too, which would, I hope, make you feel quite sick with rage and envy, if you have any decent feelings). But I do ask you to believe in this curious little drama of an autumn twilight. I can produce no photographic evidence of it, though doubtless it has its little niche in the infinite album of eternity . . . an album which most of us will peruse, when the time comes, with somewhat mixed feelings.

Here is a last footnote – or perhaps I should call it a 'tail-piece'. I took 'One' inside, and tried to soothe him with a sardine, which he ignored. Gaskin came in, and I told him what had happened.

'He's been very odd, these last weeks, in several ways,' said Gaskin, thoughtfully.

'How?'

'Well, the oddest thing of all is how he seems to be frightened of horses. He used to wait for the milkman's cart. Now
he flies under the cupboard in the scullery. And when he
hears that pony neighing in the field – why, he carries on as
though he'd seen a ghost.'

Well, perhaps he had.

CHAPTER FOURTEEN

FEMININITIES

THE reactions of the ladies of Meadowstream, when they
learned of Miss Mint's experience, were varied and
unexpected.

Miss Emily was frankly sceptical.

'Nothing like this ever happened at Merry Hall in the old
days,' she observed. 'Everything was so cheerful and healthy
and . . . and aboveboard.'

This made me feel as if I were being accused of installing
a coining machine in the cellar. 'I hope it still is.'

'Not that it has anything to do with *you*,' she added hastily.
'I merely meant that one just could not imagine it happening
in Mr. Stebbing's time. If it ever *did* happen.'

'Are you suggesting that Miss Mint invented it?'

'Oh no! Poor dear! I am sure that would be quite beyond
her capacity.'

'Or her inclination.'

'Yes, indeed. Quite. The last thing one would expect of
her. I merely meant . . .' she paused and sighed . . . 'Merry
Hall was such a very *normal* place. Just a typical English
home.'

I would have liked to retort that in a typical English home

the master of the house did not usually begin the day by playing Liszt on the pianola for the benefit of his intestines, but the remark would not have been well received.

'However,' she added, 'at least we can be thankful that Miss Mint's ghost was a reasonably amiable one. Otherwise it would have been so upsetting for your poor cats.'

It was on the tip of my tongue to tell Miss Emily about the strange episode of 'One' and the phantom gate, but I suspected that the poor woman had already been tried almost beyond endurance. So I left it at that.

On the following day, I discovered that Our Rose's attitude was very different. She accepted Miss Mint's story with no reservations whatsoever, and promptly adapted it to herself.

'It doesn't surprise me in the least,' she said. 'Not in the very least. I always Knew.'

'That Merry Hall was haunted?'

She gave a tinkling laugh. 'Aren't we putting it a little crudely? Such a banal word I always think – "haunted". I merely meant that there was Something. Somewhere. One either Knows. Or one doesn't Know. Don't you think?'

She did not appear to seek a definite answer to this somewhat sweeping statement.

She continued to arrange the flowers. We were sitting in the parlour at 'The Weathercocke', waiting for Miss Emily to join us for tea. The Czechoslovakian maid had set out a tray of flowers on the side-table – the remnants of the herbaceous border, some sprays of beech and bramble. As this was the first time that I had ever seen Rose at work, I watched with considerable interest.

For her arrangement she had chosen a container of considerable repulsion; it was fashioned in the shape of a wire-haired fox-terrier with a large hole in its back. One can be devoted to wire-haired fox-terriers, but not in Benares brass and not with large holes in their backs. The holes worried me. I had a dim sort of feeling that they must hurt the fox-terrier, particularly when, in addition to water, they contain large, spiky pin-holders. (I also have a dim sort of feeling that the pin-holders must hurt the flowers, too, and I use them as seldom as possible. However, that is perhaps carrying sensitivity to excess.)

Into this mixture of animal and mineral Our Rose was stuffing flowers with the master touch for which she is famous throughout these islands. She began with three red-hot pokers, a flower which is better left in the herbaceous border. It looks angry enough, even in these surroundings; when it is cut it looks positively enraged. To make matters worse, Rose had snipped the stalks very short. When she pushed them in the back, they looked like three savagely docked tails. This struck her as highly diverting.

'Ooh – what beautiful little tailey-waileys!' she crooned, sticking them harder on to the cruel pin-holders. 'Ooh – what a clever little doggie we are to have three beautiful little tailey-waileys!' She regarded me out of the corner of her eye to see how I was reacting to these pleasantries. I managed to assume a mask of amusement.

'*Most* little doggies have only got *one* beautiful little tailey-wailey!' she continued. 'But *we* have three!' She stepped back, and put her head on one side. Then she nodded to herself. 'Yes,' she whispered, suddenly tense. 'One, I think. Just one.'

One what? I longed to ask. Our Rose's mood had suddenly changed – or so she wished me to imagine. She was being the Artist. Her eyes were half-closed, and she moved towards the flower-tray as in a trance, still keeping her eyes on the fox-terrier. She extended her arm, and groped over the tray, till her fingers closed on a large cactus dahlia, with striped petals of white and purple. This she promptly decapitated, and thrust into the hole.

Her eyes opened. An ethereal smile lit up her face. She nodded. Then – as though she had suddenly remembered my presence – she turned. 'Only another moment now,' she breathed. 'Please forgive me. I'm always like this when I'm working. So silly of me!'

In a frenzy of creation she hurried forward, grasped a trail of ivy, thrust the stalk into the hole, and twined the rest of it round the fox-terrier's neck. Then, crooking her little finger, she pushed the end into its mouth. From here it promptly shot out again, as though the animal had rejected it in disgust.

'Naughty! Naughty!' she whispered, replacing the ivy. 'We mustn't do things like *that* with the lovely things that mummy puts into our mouths, must we? *There!*' She gave a final pat. She stepped back, for the final judgment.

'I don't think we could improve on that,' she murmured, modestly.

'No indeed.' Apart from pinning a small beetroot on to the fox-terrier's behind, I could think of no suitable elaborations.

'It either comes, or it doesn't, don't you think?'

'Quite.'

'That's what I really meant when we were talking about Merry Hall and Miss Mint – and *feeling* things – whether there is Something – Somewhere. It's a question of Atmosphere. Don't you agree?'

I was absolved from answering these conundrums by the arrival of Miss Emily.

§ 11

But not for long. As soon as tea was over, Rose reverted to the topic of the ghost of Merry Hall, with the evident intention of annexing it – or some of the credit for it – to herself.

'So sorry, my dear,' she said to Miss Emily, 'that you seem to think Miss Mint invented it all.'

'I never said anything of the sort,' retorted Miss Emily indignantly. 'I merely suggested that she might have been suffering from delusions.'

'Why?'

'Nothing like that has ever happened at Merry Hall before.'

'Nothing that *you* knew about, perhaps.'

'I knew everything. If there had been the least hint of anything abnormal, Mr. Stebbing would have told me.'

'But perhaps Mr. Stebbing was not sensitive.'

Miss Emily's cheeks became very pink. 'He was the *most* sensitive of men . . .' she began.

'You misunderstand me, dear. I mean sensitive in a psychic sense. Quite a different thing.'

'He did not dabble in spiritualism, if that is what you mean.'

Rose gave a gay little laugh, the sort of laugh that might be prompted by the *gaffe* of a foolish child. She turned to me. 'How difficult it is to explain these things to people who are . . . outside.'

'Outside what?' demanded Miss Emily.

'Emily *dear*! There is no need to shout at me.'

Pause. Both ladies dived for their cups of tea. Since these cups were empty, they had to make a pantomime of drinking, which resulted in a faint sound of suction on Miss Emily's part – a sound which caused Our Rose's eyebrows to raise ever so slightly.

Rose was the first to put down her cup.

'Such a fascinating subject, I always think,' she said, again addressing her remarks to me. 'I wish I had the courage to investigate it further.'

'But surely *you* are not afraid of ghosts?' snapped Miss Emily.

'It isn't a question of being afraid of ghosts, dear, it's a question of not knowing where they might lead one. If one is psychic . . .'

'But one is not psychic.'

'Not *you*,' agreed Rose, fervently. 'Oh no! Nobody would ever dream of accusing *you* of that!'

'Nor you, I should imagine.'

Rose caught her breath, as though she were about to make a very sharp retort. Then she contrived a smile. 'I'm glad I don't show it,' she said. 'I should hate to be . . . obvious. All the same, I've known that I was psychic ever since I was a little girl.'

'How? Why?'

'Well dear, my whole life – my whole work. Take my flowers.'

'What about them?'

'*I* don't arrange them.'

Miss Emily merely pursed her lips.

'It isn't *me*. How *could* it be? Think of the amount I get through, on a busy day! I should be utterly exhausted, if I weren't Helped.'

Miss Emily pursed her lips still tighter. 'I am afraid I find this rather difficult to follow.'

Rose nodded. 'Yes dear. I'm sure you do.'

This was not at all the response that Miss Emily had sought. 'Do you mean . . .' she began.

'I mean,' interrupted Rose, 'that though mine may be the *fingers* which make my arrangements, I am only the Instrument. I am being Used. Like a brush in the hand of an artist. I do not claim, and never shall claim, to be the Creator.'

'That is just as well, dear, or people might think that you had religious mania.'

Though I was accustomed to these exchanges, I felt that the atmosphere was becoming uncomfortably warm.

'Have you noticed Rose's arrangement with the fox-terrier?' I inquired.

'One could hardly fail to notice it,' snapped Miss Emily.

'I'm afraid dear Emily disapproves of it,' said Rose.

'I should hardly *dare* to disapprove of it, if what you say is true.'

'Are you suggesting . . .?'

211

'I am suggesting nothing, dear. It is you who are doing the suggesting.'

'In what way?'

'In practically every way. You seem to wish us to believe that the Archangel Gabriel has personally descended in order to stick three red-hot pokers into the . . . the back of a brass fox-terrier . . .' She paused and gulped.

There was a deadly silence. Then Rose got up, slowly walked to the electric bell – which was cunningly concealed in the middle of a warming-pan – and pressed it. Still silence. More gulping from Miss Emily.

The Czechoslovakian maid came in.

'Would you kindly take this into the hall?' said Our Rose. 'It seems to be rather in the way.'

'My *dear* Rose,' began Miss Emily, 'there is no need to . . .'

'It is not the least trouble,' interrupted Our Rose. 'The hall, Frieda, if you please. On the oak dresser.'

Frieda lifted up the fox-terrier. One of the red-hot pokers wobbled perilously, as though it were wagging its tail. Then she carried it out of the room and shut the door behind her.

Rose heaved a dramatic sigh and sank into a chair. 'And now,' she said, with a brave smile, 'we can all relax.'

Whether the ladies did, in fact, relax, I shall never know, for I decided that it was time to take my departure. For the moment, the ways of women seemed to me somewhat fatiguing.

§ III

And yet I was to learn a great deal more concerning the ways of women in the next few weeks. For Fate was about to strike a devastating blow by suddenly decreeing that Gaskin must go to hospital for a minor operation. And that led to the advent of Mrs. Fortescue.

'I think she'll suit very well,' said Gaskin, when we were

discussing these gloomy arrangements. 'She's quite the lady.'

'Oh dear!'

'Well, it's better to have a lady you can trust than a woman you can't.'

'I suppose it is.'

'She's a good cook, and she understands about the cats.'

With that I had to be content; indeed, it would have been selfish to demand more. After all, Gaskin's would be the greater ordeal – or so it seemed at the time. And anyway, it would only be for a few weeks.

Mrs. Fortescue was indeed a lady. (She is now, I should explain, happily married, and living in an extremely remote part of the British Empire where I trust my books do not circulate.) She was the widow of an officer in the Indian Army, and something seemed to have gone wrong with her pension. She was about fifty, and what is known as 'petite' . . . a word that always seems to mean so much more in England than in France. She had snow-white hair, and it is morally certain that somewhere in the background there was an admirer who told her she looked like a French marquise. (I have never been able to understand all this talk about French marquises, because the only ones I have ever met have looked like large brown spaniels, but perhaps I have moved in the wrong circles.)

Mrs. Fortescue looked back on better days. She looked back so earnestly and so constantly that she had a sort of mental crick in the neck. She was for ever referring to the time 'when I was in Indyah' – where, it seemed, her husband had held an exalted position in the Pay Corps. And, most unfortunately, she was a devoted admirer of my works.

'How nice,' I murmured at our first interview, when – in a few well-chosen phrases – she showed that she had read practically everything that I had ever written, and had apparently taken it to heart. And indeed, it did seem at the time that this coincidence might save trouble. It would at least deter her from putting on trousers, if she had ever been so inclined.

However, as it happened, this extensive study of the works of Nichols proved almost entirely disastrous. As is proved by the incident of the spiders.

It happened like this. After Mrs. Fortescue had been with me for about three weeks, I noticed that the music-room was beginning to look extremely squalid. There really was no excuse for this; it was the only room in the house, apart from my bedroom, which was being used, all the others having been shut up in Gaskin's absence. And here it was, with thick dust on the piano, and mud on the carpet, and unemptied ashtrays.

And spiders' webs on the ceiling. In particular, one very elaborate web on a beam high up over my desk, containing an enormous spider which constantly bounced up and down with an air of great malevolence.

One morning, when the spider was in an especially bouncing mood, I could bear it no longer. I called in Mrs. Fortescue.

'I think we should really do something about these spiders' webs,' I said.

Her reaction, as she looked up to the ceiling, was unexpected. She clasped her hands, and an ecstatic smile spread over her face.

'Oh!' she cried. 'Hasn't he done it beautifully?'

I did not quite understand.

'But the spidah!' she exclaimed. 'How *beautifully* he has woven it!'

I could think of nothing to say but 'Oh'.

'I *know* how you feel about spidahs,' she went on. 'That passage in *Merry Hall*, about the spidahs on the logs, when you were lighting a fire, and how you could not *enduah* the thought of burning them!'

'Yes,' I said. 'But. . . .'

But what? I wanted to say that this was a somewhat different situation. It was one thing to pick odd spiders off logs before lighting a fire – I always do and am not at all ashamed of it – but it is another to sit at one's desk, endeavouring to compose elegant phrases, under the shadow of a monster who may at another moment shoot down on a string and bite one in the back of the neck.

But how could one explain this to Mrs. Fortescue? She would have been cut to the quick; all her illusions would have been shattered. I could only grin feebly and bear it, and make plans to steal out to the pantry in the dead of night and get the long mop which Gaskin would have used. Gaskin has the kindest of hearts but he stands no nonsense from spidahs. As he once said to me, when we were discussing this abstruse problem . . . 'What about the flies?'

As the weeks dragged by, Mrs. Fortescue's delicate susceptibilities put me into a state of constant and acute embarrassment lest I might say or do something to offend her. There was always the danger, for example, that I might forget Gaskin's departure, and absent-mindedly dart into the kitchen in a state of semi-nudity. Or there might be some hair-raising moment when I encountered *her* in a similar condition. To guard against such disasters we both developed a habit of coughing, loud and long, as we moved about the house. When Mrs. Fortescue advanced down the corridor in the morning, bearing my breakfast tray, she did so to the accompaniment of a positive fusillade of coughs, that would have suggested to an outsider that she was in an advanced stage of bronchitis. And every time I went into the kitchen I prefaced my arrival by such whoopings and clearings of the throat that by the time I opened the door I could hardly speak.

Another little habit of Mrs. Fortescue's, arising from her super-sensitivity, was very disconcerting until one got used to it. This was her trick of muffling any words or phrases which had 'delicate' associations. She seemed to preface them with the letter M.

I first learned of this habit one evening when I hurried into the house, late for an appointment with an editor. I went into the music-room, but could not find him. So I put my head through the kitchen door, and asked if he had not yet arrived. 'Oh yes,' replied Mrs. Fortescue. 'He's been here nearly twenty minutes.'

'But where *is* he?'

Mrs. Fortescue lowered her eyes. 'I think,' she murmured, 'that he is mwashing his hands.'

For a moment I did not understand what she meant. Mwashing his hands? It sounded like something to do with a compost heap. Then I understood.

She was constantly talking of her own cat, whose name was Tiddles. One day I asked her whether Tiddles was a boy or a girl. Again she lowered her eyes.

'He is a mneuter,' she said.

She pronounced it as though it were spelled Minuta, and it was only just in time that I refrained from asking if Minuta was some rare breed imported from the East.

In Mrs. Fortescue's world people did not have babies, they had mbabies; and even that was going a little far; she preferred to refer, in general terms, to '*mappy events*'. Her most daring excursion into raffish conversation was when she once expressed an opinion of her next door neighbour, with whom she apparently waged unceasing warfare. 'But what can you expect from anybody with such a background?' she demanded.

'Has she such a bad background?' I asked.

'She is . . .' She paused for a moment, and then came out with it . . . 'she is millegitimate'.

However, time and the hour run through the roughest day, and at last the morning dawned when Gaskin was due to return.

'So charming it's been,' murmured Mrs. Fortescue, as she stepped into the taxi I had ordered for her. 'Such a change. Everything so agreeable.' She made me feel like an hotel proprietor saying goodbye to a duchess.

That was the last I heard of her, except for a letter, asking somewhat mysteriously after a 'garment' which she had left behind. This proved to be a pair of pink silk pyjamas which turned up in the next week's wash. I was thankful that her inquiry had to be made by correspondence, rather than by word of mouth. 'Mpyjamas' would have been so very difficult to pronounce.

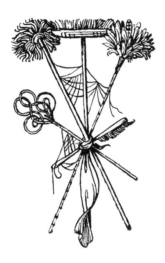

CHAPTER FIFTEEN

THE FLOWER SHOW

ACT ONE

IT was all the doing of Miss Emily and Our Rose. They crept upon me unawares, on a lovely evening in May, when I was sitting by the water garden. I am as wax in anybody's hands, in the neighbourhood of the water garden. The sight of that cool, formal sheet of silver acts on the mind like some enchanted drug. The leaves of the lilies lie so still; the tall spears of the rushes cast their shadows in the corners, a single spray of water hawthorn floats, immaculately white, regarding itself as though in a mirror. It is not only ridiculous but impossible, in such surroundings, to remember that there is an outside world, with terrifying things like Mrs. Braddock prowling about in it.

Yes, they crept upon me unawares, and before I realized it I had committed myself to the idea of a flower show at the end of June.

'We've already spoken to Mr. Pattern,' said Our Rose. (Mr. Pattern is the vicar of Great Lacing, the adjoining village.) 'He says we can have the Assembly Rooms on June 28th.'

'It's a Saturday' explained Miss Emily. 'So convenient.'

'June 28th will be very early for my lilies,' I objected. 'Couldn't we make it a fortnight later?'

'My irises would be finished,' protested Our Rose. 'And there wouldn't be a lupin left.'

'To say nothing of the roses,' added Miss Emily. 'Most of the first crop gone, and the second not even begun. All betwixt and between.'

'But wouldn't it be better to have a few really first class things rather than a little bit of everything?'

'Oh *no!*' exclaimed both ladies at once.

'Mixed bunches,' said Miss Emily firmly. 'So much more scope.'

'Much more,' agreed Our Rose. 'We both feel that very strongly.'

'The prizes would really be for artistic arrangement.'

'Yes indeed.' Our Rose nodded emphatically. 'It's high time that people in Meadowstream were shaken out of the rut.'

Oh dear! Why this passion for shaking people out of ruts? I am devoted to ruts. Moreover, most of the people who are in ruts are much nicer, and much happier, than the people who are not. To speak of ruts as though they were undesirable is the sign of a coarse and callow mind. Ruts are the wise old wrinkles that civilization has traced on the earth's ancient face. However, one could not explain such things to Our Rose.

'And who were you going to get to judge?' I asked.

'But *you,* of course!' exclaimed both ladies simultaneously.

I was taken aback. 'Oh dear! I don't think I could do anything like that.'

'But why not?'

'I don't think I'm qualified.'

'Nonsense.'

'Besides . . .' I hesitated, trying to think of an excuse. My real reason, of course, was that if Rose were to enter the competition she would consider herself grossly insulted if she were not automatically given the first prize. And I utterly abominated everything she had ever done in the way of flower decoration. Those daffodils with their heads chopped off! Shall I ever forget them? Those poor irises, forced into an almost horizontal position, with their stalks pushed into a sort of inverted pin-cushion! Worst of all, those ghastly china ornaments which she was always sticking into her arrangements ... nasty little Dresden shepherdesses peeping through a cluster of asparagus fern, repulsive little Chinamen leering behind bits of apple-blossom. She had once even bought some of those alarming blue brooches that are made of butterflies' wings – (how fortunate that our temperate climate saves us from these horrors!) – and had wired them to the spikes of delphiniums.

'Besides what?' demanded Rose.

There was nothing for it but to lie, even if it choked me. 'Besides, if you are competing yourself, well ... the result's a foregone conclusion.'

'How absurd!' Rose gave a little tinkling laugh. 'I should only do something terribly simple.'

Yes, I thought to myself. Madonna lilies chopped in half, floating in a bowl of mayonnaise, with four india-rubber ducks lurking in the background.

'It would be so vulgar, don't you think, to do anything ostentatious? Like wearing all one's jewels to a village concert?'

Those would be the garnets, I thought.

'However,' she added archly, 'perhaps if I made a special effort you might give me an honourable mention!'

Miss Emily was beginning to feel out of the conversation. She cleared her throat and produced a small note-book. 'We thought we ought to have one or two simple rules,' she said. 'The first rule would be that no bunch must contain any flower that has been *bought*.'

'Quite.'

'Next, we thought that no flowers should be used that have not come out of our *own* gardens.'

'Won't that make it rather hard on people like Miss Mint?' I asked. 'Her garden's hardly started yet.'

'Couldn't she do something with wild flowers?'

'That would put her at rather a disadvantage.'

'Perhaps we might make an exception in the case of Miss Mint,' suggested Our Rose.

'My dear, once we start making exceptions we shall never stop.'

'Personally,' I said, 'I think we might allow people to borrow from each other.'

'You know what that will mean, of course,' replied Rose. 'It will mean that for at least a week before the show Erica will go charging about through everybody's gardens like a raging hyena, stripping them completely bare.'

'I hardly think it will be as bad as that.'

'There is nothing I would put beyond her – *nothing*!' There was a moment's pause. Then a gleam came into Rose's eye. 'Wait a moment, I think I have an idea. Yes! I know exactly what I shall say to her. I shall say that all my flowers, unfortunately, are grown for sale. And that it would therefore be useless for her to buy any – not, of course, that she ever *would*! – because she would be forbidden to use any of them!'

'But surely, dear,' said Miss Emily, 'that would apply equally to yourself? If your flowers are grown for sale, you would not be able to use them, either!'

'I should say that they were grown for sale to others, dear,' retorted Rose, with some warmth. 'Quite different, you see.'

'No dear, I'm afraid I don't. Stupid of me, of course, but I should have thought that if the flowers are grown for sale at all . . .'

'For sale to *others*. How can I sell flowers to myself?' demanded Rose, on a rising tone.

'I really don't know, dear. But you are so clever that sometimes I think you could sell flowers to anybody or anything.'

By now a dangerous gleam had come into Our Rose's eye.

'Don't you think, dear, that you are being a teeny bit dense?'

'Yes dear. I'm sure I am. But I still think that a seller implies a buyer.'

'But if there *is* no buyer . . .'

'Then I fail to see how there can be any sale!' retorted Miss Emily, triumphantly. Before Our Rose could reply she turned to me, and in trembling tones observed: 'Sometimes people who are very business-like do not always see the *simple* things.'

'This is not a question of being business-like . . .' began Our Rose.

'No dear. You have made that *quite* obvious . . .' began Miss Emily.

And how the argument might have ended, if it had been allowed to continue, I dare not guess. But at that moment it was brought to an abrupt conclusion by the arrival of Marius.

§ 11

I have never been more glad to see him. Both ladies stand somewhat in awe of Marius, and, as a result, are usually on their best behaviour in his presence. So it was on this occasion. Frowns were banished, feathers were preened, all again was smiles and sweetness.

'You will be entering, of course?' asked Miss Emily, when she had told him about the show.

'I am not sure.'

'Oh but you *must*!' pleaded Our Rose. 'I have never forgotten that delicious arrangement you made with the acanthus leaves.'

'That was a copy from a frieze at Knossus.'

'So much the better!'

'Yes, but it was only composed of leaves. There were no flowers in it. I do not expect that most people would like it. Except, of course, the Zulus.'

Rose nodded. 'Yes. Of course. The Zulus.' She had not the faintest idea what he was talking about, but on all matters connected with flowers she likes to appear omniscient.

'What have the Zulus got to do with it?' inquired Miss Emily, suspiciously.

Our Rose hesitated. Then she said: 'It is a question of how they *feel*, dear. About flowers. The Zulus, you know. All rather difficult to explain. You see . . .'

'If you will forgive me for saying so,' interrupted Marius, 'it is not in the least difficult to explain. They merely hate them.'

Our Rose nodded vigorously. 'Hate them,' she echoed.

'Why?' Miss Emily addressed her remark directly to Our Rose.

But Marius – who had now gathered that Rose's knowledge of the floral reactions of the Zulus was less thorough than she pretended – came gallantly to her rescue.

'They hate them – as Rose would tell you – because they cannot eat them.'

'Quite' said Rose. 'None of them.'

'They call them "the weeds that stink",' continued Marius. 'It is a very natural reaction, in a primitive society. They see these tempting objects, with their sweet smells and their lovely shapes, displayed on every bough of the forest, as though they were arranged for a feast. And when they try to swallow them, they are bitter and burning. I hope you are not expecting a very large attendance of Zulus at your fête?'

Rose assured him that they would be in a minority.

'That is fortunate,' said Marius. 'They would almost certainly wreck it.'

With which pleasantry the ladies took their departure, and I was left to tell Marius the story of the spider. I need hardly add that he produced, out of the hat, an entire troupe of historical spiders . . . the spider that had annoyed Voltaire, so that he killed it with the words 'Ecrasez L'Infame' . . . the spider that had solved a problem in theology for Erasmus . . . the spider that had caused a panic at the court of Catherine the Great.

'But of course,' he said, 'the most exciting of all spiders is in our immediate vicinity.'

I sat up with a start and looked around me.

'There is no cause for alarm,' added Marius, with a smile. 'It is – or should be – in the pool. Shall we go and see?'

We walked over to the edge, and peered into the clear water. In a few moments Marius had found what he was seeking. 'Come here,' he said softly. I went to his side. There, on the floor of the pool, was a small black object, waving its legs as though it were grappling with something. Each time that it moved, a large silver bubble moved with it. Then the movement stopped, and suddenly the bubble, accompanied by the spider, floated to the surface. The bubble broke, there was a little ripple, and the spider scuttled rapidly to the shelter of the reeds.

'I wonder how many million years it took to learn that lesson,' said Marius.

And then he explained to me the miracle of the water-spider. Like all the best miracles, it is dramatically simple. When the water-spider feels that it is time to dine, it blows a large bubble, which it holds under one of its arms, as if it were holding the ball in water-polo. From the edge of the bank it then selects a piece of grit or sand, grips on to it, and sinks to the bottom – the grit acting as ballast. It then proceeds to dine. Having dined, it holds tightly to the bubble, lets go of the grit, and shoots to the top, as though in an elevator. Of all the fantasies ever evolved by the celestial scientists, working so high above us in their cloudy laboratories, this is surely one of the most delightful.

§ III

The days sped by without any further intrusions, and I had almost forgotten about the flower show, when one day Miss Mint arrived, at about tea time, bearing with her a pamphlet for my approval.

A

GRAND FLOWER SHOW

will be held at

GREAT LACING ASSEMBLY ROOMS

on

SATURDAY, JUNE 28TH

All residents of Great Lacing and Meadowstream are cordially invited to send exhibits of flowers

grown in their own gardens

Special Prizes **will be awarded for MIXED FLOWER ARRANGEMENTS**

The Show will be opened at 3 o'clock by

MR. BEVERLEY NICHOLS

who will act as the judge and distribute the prizes at 6 p.m.

Among those who have already promised to exhibit are

The Hon. Emily Kaye
Miss Erica Wyman
Mr. Marius Lancaster
The Rev. Charles Pattern
Dr. Harley Garson

AND

ROSE FENTON

'Miss Fenton has made me the secretary,' she explained, in a timorous voice. 'So very kind . . . the remuneration, which she insists on paying herself, will be most useful . . . though I fear . . .' She shook her head in foreboding, though what her fears might be she did not choose to define.

Well, that was nice of Rose, I thought, though perhaps a little premature. She was a generous creature, and it would not be the first time that she had given Miss Mint a helping hand. Then I studied the pamphlet, and Rose's generosity appeared in a slightly different light.

My immediate reaction, on studying this document, was one of acute apprehension. What Emily would say to AND ROSE FENTON I dared not imagine. To put her name in block capitals was bad enough, to preface it by the dramatic AND was worse, to omit the title of Miss, as though she were a sort of Margot Fonteyn, was worst of all. At the very least there would be squalls; there might be hurricanes.

However, it would not do to let Miss Mint see my anxiety; her little world was already so full of fears and forebodings that it would be a crime to add to them. So I merely said:

'Has this pamphlet been passed for publication?'

'Oh yes! Indeed, it *has* been published. Five hundred copies. Miss Fenton is busy making out lists of people to whom we shall send it.'

'I wonder why she didn't show it to me first?'

'Oh dear! Is there anything *wrong* with it?' Miss Mint gazed at me in such alarm, and clasped and unclasped her small hands in such an access of nervousness, that I hastened to reassure her. After all, what was done, was done. One could only cross one's fingers and hope for the best.

'Not at all. It looks very well.'

'Are you *sure?*'

'Quite sure. It says all that is needed.'

It did. And a great deal more.

So I gave it back to Miss Mint, and she rose to go.

As she took her departure she looked around her, at the green lawns, and the old walls, on which the roses were already blooming.

'So beautiful,' she murmured. Then a deep sigh. 'And so sad, when one thinks of the evenings drawing in.'

'But Miss Mint, we are only in the middle of May. The evenings are drawing *out*.'

'Yes. But in five weeks time they begin to draw in again. Had you forgotten that?'

'Frankly, for the moment, I had.'

She shook her head. 'I can never forget it. Every time we come to December the twentieth I say to myself "In six months time the evenings will begin to draw in again".'

'Miss Mint, that is positively morbid.'

'I'm sure it is. But surely you'd realized that I *am* a very morbid person?'

She looked at me with a timid smile. But in spite of the shadow in her eyes, there was also a twinkle in them.

'In that case, let me pick you a bunch of flowers and you will feel better.'

She held up her hand. 'No. Please don't. You will be needing them all for the show.'

This was so absurd a suggestion that I paid no heed to it, and picked her a nice bunch from the herbaceous border.

But as I bent low among the paeonies, looking from them to the first blue spires of the irises, and on to the columbines, and wondering how they would all mix, and whether I ought to add one or two sprays from the *clematis montana* on the wall, I suddenly realized that Miss Mint had unconsciously presented me with the excuse that I had been seeking all my life . . . the excuse for which every gardener must have groped, at some time or other, in the back of his mind . . . the excuse which will enable him, with a clear conscience, NOT to strip his borders for the benefit of others.

I should say that they were being saved for a flower show!

If you do not own a garden, or if – as is very likely – you are repelled by these ungenerous sentiments, you would be wise to skip the rest of this chapter. But if you too have suffered from the predatory instincts of your friends, you will perhaps be inclined to read on.

It may sound terrible – indeed it *does* sound terrible – to suggest that one begrudges giving flowers to friends. One doesn't, provided that they are the right flowers, and that one has time to think about them, and prowl out to the kitchen garden to investigate the cutting beds, and scramble up behind the guelder rose bushes with a pair of secateurs, to cut off the back branches. And provided that one is not fussed and rushed about it all.

But one always *is* fussed and rushed about it all, particularly by a woman. She swallows her last cocktail, and then she says she must go, and gives you the LOOK WHICH CAN ONLY MEAN ONE THING. That thing is the entire contents of the herbaceous border.

'What a *mass* of flowers you have!' she sighs, gazing hungrily across the lawn. 'Look at those paeonies alone! Do you know how much a single paeony costs in London?'

As soon as this question is asked, one knows how the rest of the dialogue will go. A single paeony, she will tell you, costs the earth. A few paeonies, she continues, would make all the difference in her life. Finally she suggests that one's own paeonies are so overcrowded that if they are not thinned out they will throttle themselves. If I have heard this argument once I have heard it a hundred times. Do you recognize it? Listen. . . .

'Two shillings!' she cries. That's what they want for *one* in that shop in Bond Street. What can one *do*?'

I cannot think what she can do. Nor what I can do, either. I only know that I have not the least desire to do it.

'And they *are* so exquisite, and they last so long!'

As though by invisible wires, one finds oneself being slowly

drawn across the lawn, towards the paeonies. And that is the beginning of the end.

All this, as I suggested before, must sound the ultimate in stinginess to those who do not own a garden. How can one explain – especially to a woman – that it is not really stingy at all? How can one make her understand that a clump of paeonies, to the man who has grown them, is not merely a clump of paeonies, a group of flowers waiting to be cut, and stuffed into a vase in Bruton Street on top of a shiny Bluthner piano. A clump of paeonies, to its owner, is something that is deeply rooted in his heart. These flowers are part of himself. It is not only a question of their crowning moment, the moment in June when they crowd up to the sky in an ivory ecstasy of blossom. There have been long months, and maybe years, of training for that moment. The owner of those paeonies has slaved for them, sacrificed himself for them, sometimes, I think, taken years off his life for them. They are not just 'for cutting'. They are for living with, and maybe for dying with, too.

But women will never understand. They come down, and they see a bunch in the music-room that is like a firework display. Lovely and vulgar and blazing and opulent, with vivid branches of this and that shooting out in all directions, and scarlet cascades of Love-lies-bleeding, and shimmering backgrounds of silver centaurea and Lord knows what else. They think they've only got to be let loose in the herbaceous border to achieve the same result. Which is of course grotesque.

The making of that bunch may have taken the better part of a day. It has meant prowling round a group of lupins from North, South, East and West, and then, after five minutes deliberation, picking just one. It has meant walking a quarter of a mile into the orchard for one spray of dark-leaved prunus, a quarter of a mile back again, and then, as likely as not, a repeat journey, because the spray proves to be the wrong shape. It has meant climbing inside thickets of syringa, and

231

mounting on steps to reach hidden sprays of lilac, and making raids on the back shelf of the greenhouse to pick the one freak amaryllis that is six weeks too late. Every shade of colour, every twist of leaf and stem, is the result of the most intimate knowledge of which only the gardener himself knows the secret. And then some women think that they can come down with a pair of shears and rush about like a lot of maddened zebras without causing havoc and destruction!

But there, I have said enough, and probably far too much. It only remains to add that for people like Miss Mint – who has been standing by us, all this time, in the lengthening shadows – there will always be flowers, while I am here to pick them. I like to think that they will help her to forget that her evenings are 'drawing in'.

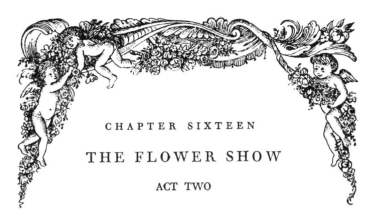

CHAPTER SIXTEEN

THE FLOWER SHOW

ACT TWO

THE storm was not long in breaking. On the very next morning, just when I was trying to get down to work, Miss Emily's car swept down the lane, and stopped with a sharp grinding of brakes. She ran up the steps so swiftly, pressed the bell with such force, beat such a loud tattoo with her toe, and generally made so much commotion, that it was impossible to deny her. So I answered the door and let her in.

She walked straight past me into the drawing-room, breathing heavily. Instead of sitting down, she stood very erect, and undid the clasp of her bag.

'I've brought you something that you ought to see,' she snapped.

'I believe I can guess what it is.'

'Oh!' She hesitated, and gave me a gimlet look. Then she drew the Flower Show pamphlet out of her bag and thrust it towards me.

'Yes. I thought that would be it.'

Another 'Oh!' and another gimlet look.

'I'd like to assure you,' I added, 'that I only saw it for the first time last night, and that I had nothing whatever to do with the writing of it.'

'Thank heavens!' Miss Emily sat down sharply on the sofa,

and heaved a dramatic sigh. 'Not that I ever suspected for a moment that you were concerned in it. But with that woman, one never knows. Could you have *conceived* she would do anything like this?'

'The word AND is certainly rather unfortunate.'

'Quite.' Miss Emily nodded vigorously. 'The word AND. I never knew any word could sound so offensive. AND! Monstrous! AND Rose Fenton! As though she were going to come on in spangles, riding a white poodle at the end of the last act. If it were BUT it would be more to the point!'

I tried to pour a speck of oil on the seething waters.

'Perhaps other people may not notice it so much.'

'How can they help noticing it? She's plastered it all over the county.'

'Surely not already?'

'Well, there are three outside the Assembly Rooms. And one at the blacksmith's and one in the window of the Post Office at the corner. What people will imagine I do *not* know.'

I had a suspicion that people would imagine what they usually imagined in this part of the world. Which is precious little.

'Of course,' continued Miss Emily, 'I shall resign.'

'Please don't do that!'

'I'm sorry; I've no alternative.'

'But if you resign, the vicar will feel that he ought to resign too. And half the others. The whole thing will become a farce.'

'Rose has done her best to make it one already.'

'Perhaps she has. All the same, I think we ought to try to rise above it. I must, whatever happens. After all, I'm the judge.'

'So you are.' Miss Emily nodded thoughtfully. 'I'd almost forgotten, with all these distractions.' A curious gleam came into her eyes. 'Of course, as judge, you *would* be in a position to . . .'

'To what?'

Miss Emily gave a nervous laugh. 'Oh, never mind! I mustn't put ideas into your head.'

More she would not say, and there, for the moment, the matter rested, with Miss Emily promising to be very noble and to rise above it.

But she *had* put an idea into my head. A disturbing idea. It seemed that I was cast for the role of mediator in a struggle of life and death between Miss Emily and Our Rose, and that whatever decision I made would incur the lasting enmity of either one or the other, and probably both.

§ I I

And now, another threat began to loom up on the horizon. My lilies were not coming out!

As I was not a competitor this might seem to be a matter of minor consequence. However, the lilies had so much *réclame* that I had promised to arrange a big bunch of them in the hall, and if this promise was not fulfilled I should look very foolish. It would not matter with people like Rose and Emily and Marius; they knew that the lilies were in fact as fabulous as rumour proclaimed them. But it would matter very much with the general public, who, thanks to the local press, were preparing to go into ecstasies about them.

I did not realize this till a bare fortnight before the date of the show, to be precise, on June 14th. I had gone out to the lily bed after dinner, and was prowling along beside them, when I suddenly thought: 'But this is extraordinary. There isn't a single gleam of white anywhere. Not one of them has begun to open.'

I called out to Oldfield, who was pottering about near the greenhouse, watering his verbenas.

'Oldfield. Aren't these lilies rather late?'

He ambled over. 'Aye. They're late all right. They're nigh on three weeks late.'

'But what's happened?'

'Nowt. That's what's happened.'

'I don't understand you.'

He heaved a deep sigh. 'There's been no sun. There's been no rain. There's been nowt. Nowt but long grey days with nowt in 'em.' It might have been Uncle Vanya speaking.

'But this is terrible. The flower show's on June 28th.'

Oldfield gave a very significant sniff. 'I know nowt about t'flower show', he observed.

I realized that I had made a grave mistake in not taking him into my confidence.

'I thought perhaps I had mentioned it,' I began. But it was quite impossible to be untruthful with Oldfield. So I said, rather feebly, that there had always been so much else to talk about.

Oldfield put down his watering can, and folded his arms. 'Doovz,' he proclaimed, 'didn't hold with flower shows.'

'No. But all the same . . .'

'Doovz,' he went on, relentlessly, 'said they was more bother than they was worth.'

'Perhaps they are. But . . .'

'Mister Doov,' he continued, 'said that if you get t'prizes, they never forgive it. And that if you don't get t'prizes, they never forget it.'

'I wasn't really thinking of the prizes . . .'

'And Mr. Stebbing,' he boomed on, 'said he didn't want no seconds. If he couldn't get t'firsts, he wanted nowt. I could have got him all t'firsts he wanted, only he wasn't taking no risks.'

'I should have thought these lilies would have got a first anywhere.'

'Aye. They would. But when?' He began to potter down the row, occasionally taking a bud between his old fingers, and grunting to himself.

'They want a week of sun,' he said. 'And they want a couple of days of rain.'

'Would watering help?'

'Aye, t'would help. But whose a'going to do it?'

'I could come out with the hose . . .'

'T'hose!' He snorted contemptuously. 'If you go putting cold tap water on these you'll set 'em back all t'more. They wants soft water from butts, at proper temperature.'

We might have stood there till nightfall discussing ways and means if Gaskin had not come out from the house to say that I was wanted on the telephone. It was a long and boring conversation, at the end of which I found myself committed to a whole new pile of work. Work, work, work . . . there would be no time for watering the lilies. I had better go to my desk right away.

It was after eleven when I laid down my pen. I looked out of the window. It was a clear, cool night with a thin moon rising. Suddenly, across the lawn I saw the shadow of a man walking. He drew nearer, and as he passed from the darkness of the shrubbery I saw that it was Oldfield. He was walking very slowly, he was more bent than usual, and he looked dog-tired.

Was it possible?

I unlocked the conservatory door and hurried out to the old walled kitchen garden. Yes, it *was* possible! From the lily bed came the sweet scent of freshly watered earth, the soil was dark and drenched, and all down the path were trickles of water that glistened in the moonlight. For the last two hours the old man must have been up and down, bearing nigh on a hundred cans of water, stooping over the water butts, dragging up the heavy cans . . . and all at the end of a long day's work, at an age when most men of his years would long ago have been tucked up in bed.

I found myself smiling, out there in the silent garden, at the thought of the sheer goodness and sweetness of some

237

people. And though I have said it before, I will risk saying it again – 'they don't make that sort any more, not nowadays'.

§ I I I

Outside the garden, however, the 'sheer goodness and sweetness of some people' was not always conspicuous. For although no open warfare had been declared between the two main combatants, there were numerous reports of minor skirmishes and what might be called 'frontier incidents'. Thus, at one party, Miss Emily had introduced Our Rose to an American visitor, in clear and ringing tones, as Miss AND Fenton. The American, unaware of the mesh of intrigue by which he was surrounded, naturally assumed that 'Andfenton' was indeed her name, and since Americans have a passion for people's names, which they constantly repeat, like toastmasters at a banquet, Miss 'Andfenton' she remained for the rest of the party.

Apart from these cold war reports, there were rumours of a pleasanter nature, concerning the plans which the various competitors were making for our delight. Miss Mint, it seemed, had conceived the idea of a nest of rose-buds, lined with moss, and filled with blackbirds' eggs, over which she proposed to scatter single blossoms of anchusa. It sounded as gay as could be, but I could not help wondering if the principal egg would bear the mystic letters N.W.H. Marius, I gathered, was proposing to make a bunch entirely composed of flowers with classical associations. 'It will look remarkably hideous,' he informed me, with a bland smile, 'and it will smell repulsive. But it may refresh some people's memories with a few legends of their schooldays. I shall begin, I think, with a spray of *arbutus unedo*, in honour of Pliny.'

'What had Pliny to do with it?'

'He made a very charming pun upon its name. *Unedo*, of

course, means I Eat One. And Pliny said that it was called this because nobody in his senses would ever want to eat two. In case you have forgotten I should remind you that it was one of the fruits which which Polyphemus tried to tempt Galatea.'

'What else will you put in?'

'Some parsley, I think. The Greeks would have thought us very odd for putting parsley on our plates instead of on our heads. When Horace made a wreath for Phyllis, he chose parsley. But please do not tell Rose, or she will get up to some terrible tricks with vegetables.'

'And then?'

'Certainly some leaves of the hellebore, in case passions run too high. Do you remember your Dioscorides? No? That is not surprising, nobody does. It is a pity, because he was a very colourful person. He recommended hellebore for four morbid conditions – epileptical, melancholic, frantic and paralytical. It might not be wise, however, to take his advice. Hellebore is a deadly poison. It even nearly killed a saint.'

'Which one?'

'St. Martin. Whenever I pass St. Martin's in the Fields, I have a feeling that I may see a clump of hellebore sprouting at the foot of the Nelson Column.'

Epileptical, melancholic, frantic and paralytical . . . as yet, our moods were not quite so violent. But things were warming up.

§ I V

Friday, June 27th, the day before the Show, was a scorcher. The sun was pitiless, the sky like a tight-stretched drum. After breakfast 'One' and 'Four' retired to the shelter of a clump of delphiniums, and sank into the shadows, reminding me of jellies that had not quite set. 'Five', the indefatigable, walked slowly out to the edge of the pool, dabbed a languid paw at one water-beetle, and then subsided into a cluster of spiraea.

I longed to spend the day in the garden, but there were a number of things to be done in the neighbourhood, so I decided to get them over as early as possible. Soon after nine I was driving down the lane on the way to the station, to call for some water-fleas that had arrived the night before.

Here, to my surprise, I encountered Our Rose. She was at the booking office, buying a day return to Waterloo. By her side was a large suitcase. For the moment she did not see me, and when I wished her good morning, she gave a nervous start.

'You look as if you were running away.'

Was it my fancy or did her cheeks flush a deeper red than was warranted by the heat?

'So tiresome,' she mumured, 'having to go up to London.'

'Business?'

'What else could it be on a day like this?'

'You've not forgotten about tomorrow, I hope?'

'Tomorrow?' She frowned, as though she were searching her memory. Then she gave a forced laugh. 'Oh – you mean our little flower show? I must certainly try to look in some time during the day.'

I began to feel dismayed. 'But we're counting on you to do something quite wonderful.'

'Oh really – what nonsense! I'm so rushed that I'm not sure if I shall be able to do anything at all.'

'But you *must*. Even if it's just a few roses arranged in any old way it would be better than nothing.'

Rose gave me a frosty smile. 'I'm afraid I'm not very good at arranging roses in any old way. You should ask dear Emily. She does that sort of thing quite beautifully.'

'I'm so sorry,' I began. 'All I meant . . .'

'Not at all,' she interrupted. 'I quite understand. I expect dear Emily will stagger us tomorrow. She's probably been up all night, as it is. Yes. Almost certainly. At this very moment I expect that she's half covered in sand, with her hair full of barbed wire netting.'

240

She gripped her suitcase and glanced at the clock. 'I must fly.'

'Let me carry that for you.'

'Please don't bother. It's quite empty.' She bit her lip, as though she had said something she regretted. 'At least, there's nothing heavy in it.'

She flashed me a dubious smile, and hurried on to the platform.

§ v

The water-fleas were in two large tins, which had to be carried very-carefully, and arranged on the bottom of the car, wedged in by newspapers lest they should be spilt.

For the moment, the contemplation of these fascinating creatures, and the moral problems with which they invariably confronted me, took my mind off the painful scene which had just been enacted.

I prized open one of the lids and peered inside. Yes, there they were, tens of thousands of them in the clear water, tiny black specks, darting about in a state of the utmost excitement. Why? Was it fear that animated them, or was it some strange ecstasy of creation? Whatever it might be, I was about to destroy them in the most ruthless manner, by casting them into the pool, where they would be devoured by the goldfish, who must appear to them to be many times the size of whales.

It was all most complex and difficult. The people in the shop had assured me that the goldfish were growing sluggish because of an insufficiency of water-fleas, which act on their systems like a sort of cocktail. When I talked about it to the very nice young saleswoman, she seemed to take it all as a matter of course; there was no suggestion that we were, in fact, planning murder on a scale which would have staggered Nero. Yet, what else were we doing?

Besides, what did one really *know* about water-fleas? What right had one to assume that they could be slaughtered like this, without danger either to one's immortal soul, or to theirs? One of those water-fleas might be, in its own sphere, a Shakespeare or a Michelangelo, or more possibly a Gracie Fields. In that teeming multitude there might be Miltonic water-fleas, Chopinesque water-fleas, tiny creatures that were destined to be the Newtons of Water-Fleadom. And here one was, casting them all to a loathsome death.

And here one was, too, at the pool, lifting the cans and pouring the fleas into their grave. The ripples die down, the fleas disappear, there is a moment's pause. And then, from behind the irises, there is a flash of gold, and another and another, and the goldfish dance around, to enjoy their cocktail. The massacre has begun. Well, thank God it is soon over. The goldfish, at least, enjoyed it. What was death for one was life for the other. Which is one of the few meagre consolations which occur to the thinking man when he is dizzied by the eternal see-saw of the universe.

§ VI

The morning was still young, and though the heat was fiercer than ever, I must continue my journeys. This time I was bound for the pleasant country town of Kenton, in order to purchase a number of still more deadly weapons of war, such as nicotine dust with which to powder the tops of the new pines. (Memo. It must be put on very carefully, or we should have a repetition of the awful occasion when 'One' licked some of it off the lower branches and was poisoned.) Also weedkiller. Not arsenic, because even when you ask for arsenic weedkiller you go scarlet in the face and feel like Crippen. At least I do. I only once bought some arsenic weedkiller, and when it was mixed, it was quite horrifying; it had a colour of indescribable evil, a sort of pale pink with a tinge of green, a colour of corruption and deceit and death. I poured the mixture through a grating in the lane, and needless to say that quiet thoroughfare suddenly became alive with all sorts of inquisitive urchins who wondered what was going on. Then I gave the remains of the tin to Oldfield and told him to bury it good and deep, and never to say where he had put it.

Then there were nicer things, like bass and bonemeal, and a new and much advertised fertilizer which apparently made flowers shoot up as though they had been planted in a conjurer's hat. And a patent sort of potting machine, which Oldfield would despise, and sniff at, and somehow contrive to make a failure.

These exertions had earned me a moment's relaxation, so I decided to stroll down the street to the little flower-shop at the corner, to see what they had in the window. There is often a somewhat malicious satisfaction in looking into the windows of flower-shops, if one has a garden, and seeing how much one does *not* have to pay for very inferior specimens of one's own flowers.

So I walked along, and then, just before reaching the shop, I came to an abrupt halt. For there, by the kerb, stood Miss Emily's car. And there, inside the window, bending over a large bowl of exceptionally fine gladioli, was Miss Emily herself.

I stepped back into the entrance of the book-shop next door, and waited. Developments were swift. Miss Emily plucked out a dozen gladioli, turned to a bowl of tiger-lilies, nodded to the assistant, went over to a bowl of ixias, nodded again, and disappeared. Shadows passed and repassed over the glass, indicating great activity. Then there was the tinkle of a bell, as the door opened, and out she staggered, loaded with a positive blaze of blossom. There was a great deal of bowing and scraping as the assistant helped her into the car. To which she was certainly entitled, for she must have spent several pounds.

Well, that, as they say, was that. Something sinister was evidently brewing. Miss Emily, spending a small fortune on flowers . . . Our Rose, speeding to London with an empty suitcase. It could all add up to But One Thing. There was thunder in the air.

There was indeed, in more senses than one. During this little scene the skies had been darkening, and a hot wind had blown down the street. A low roar echoed from the skies. The storm was upon us.

§ V I I

On the way home, driving through torrents of rain, to the accompaniment of a sinister roar of atmospheric drums, I neared Miss Mint's cottage. It might be a kindness to call and see her. She was a little creature who shrivelled at the approach of violence. This was a very violent moment; there was madness in the air; and she was all alone.

As soon as she opened the door I could see that she was terrified; she winced with every flash of lightning, and led me into a room which was in semi-darkness, for she had drawn the curtains.

'So kind of you to call,' she murmured. 'Do you think it foolish of me to have drawn the curtains?'

'No. I think it's a very good idea.'

'All these trees round the house. Perhaps I ought to have them cut down?'

'I don't think they're near enough to do any harm.'

'I should hate to cut down a tree merely because I had been a coward.'

Another livid flash, and a crack like the blow of a fist.

'It isn't cowardice,' I said. 'It's just that you feel things very acutely.'

'I suppose I do.' She was pressing her small hands together

244

till the knuckles were white. It was obviously an effort for her to talk.

Behind her was an old Victorian pier-glass. She had thrown a patchwork quilt over it. She noticed that I was looking at it.

'My father always used to cover up the mirrors when there was a storm,' she explained, as though she were trying to excuse herself.

'Yes. Lots of people did.'

'He used to run round the house, tearing the sheets off the beds and draping them round every mirror he could find. And he used to cover up the knives and the forks too, if there was a storm when we were dining. He was a big, strong man, but he was very . . .' she hesitated for the right word . . . 'very easily upset. One summer night, when I was a child, we were in the dining-room, and a storm came on quite suddenly. And he sprang up and pulled the tablecloth on to the floor, just as it was, with the knives and the dishes and the glasses and the flowers, and made a great bundle of it, and pushed it under the table. I was very frightened, with all the broken glass, and the wine showing red through the white cloth.'

'I'm not surprised.'

'He did it for the best,' she protested. 'He told me stories, to warn me. Once he told me about a man who had been struck by lightning on a golf course. He said that the man had been found with his legs twisted round his neck.' She gave a little laugh, in which there was a note of hysteria. 'Right round his neck! I've never forgotten that, whenever there is a storm, and . . .'

She did not finish the sentence. A searing flash finished it for her. She dropped her head and covered her face with her hands. In the roar that followed I seemed to hear the ugly snarl of the drunken brute who had been her father – the lumbering hulk who had been so 'easily upset' that his tirades had struck terror into all around him, and had left his children with only one legacy, the legacy of fear. And I thought of all the other women there must be, lonely, ageing women, sitting in darkened rooms, hearing in the uproar of the elements the echoes of their unhappy childhood.

Never again would I smile when I read those mystic letters 'N.W.H.'. There was more in them for tears than for laughter.

But now the fury of the storm was passing; the lightning became less frequent, the thunder roared less harshly. I heard a timid voice asking if I would like a glass of elderberry wine. Yes, I said, I should like it very much. Which was quite untrue, for though elderberry wine is a most melodious title, though it has a music which would have delighted Keats, it is, in practice, like extremely disgusting invalid port. However, I drank it with a will, on this occasion, out of a thin and elegant sherry glass, in tribute to a brave little lady who had nobody to care for her.

When I left, the curtains were drawn back again, to admit a few pallid rays of sunlight. There was a smile on Miss Mint's face, even if it was only a flickering one.

'N.W.H.?' I said.

She blushed, and shook her head. 'You shouldn't laugh at an old lady.'

'You're not an old lady. And I'm not laughing, anyway.'

She took my hand. 'N.W.H.' she whispered.

§ VIII

We did not hear the last of the storm till the end of the day. It finally blew itself out while I was having dinner – spaghetti, garnished with freshly chopped onions, topped with grated Parmesan cheese, and washed down with a glass of cheap Spanish wine. Price, including wine, about two shillings and three pence.

I decided to walk round to the Assembly Rooms to see how

things were getting on. Although a few of the competitors would not be bringing their flowers till the morning, most of the exhibits were already in their places, and it would be helpful to have a private view of them. Apart from that, I wanted to arrange my own lilies, of which Oldfield had carried up a magnificent bunch, picked before the breaking of the storm. When I asked him how he thought they looked, he replied, with a cavernous sigh, that they were 'not oop to mooch'. This phrase, translated into normal terms, meant that they were of superlative quality, which was comforting.

It was growing dark when I reached the hall. I was surprised to find the door open, and a light burning inside. However, nobody seemed to be about, so I could wander round and inspect the arrangements at my leisure. There were nearly fifty of them, mostly of a high standard. People had brought their most precious vases, and had filled them with the greatest ingenuity and taste; some of the most delicate arrangements had been created by people whom one would never had credited with any artistic inclinations . . . an enormous blood-stained woman whom I had often noticed at the butcher's in a neighbouring village had contrived a design which might have come from the fingers of Puck; it was made of trailing honeysuckle and sprays of Queen Anne's lace – which some people call Cow's Parsley. A gigantic young man from the garage, who looked as though he could lift a car in one hand and throw it across the road, had made a tiny quilt of pansies, sunk into a tray of water, and hanging down over the sides so that it looked like a patchwork tablecloth.

Neither Miss Emily nor Our Rose had yet brought their exhibits; they were evidently reserved to stagger us at the last moment. Miss Mint's bird's-nest, however, was there, so pretty that it would certainly merit some sort of award. And Marius's classical bunch, which was striking though somewhat unorthodox, as it appeared to consist almost entirely of vegetables. I must remember to ask him what they all meant.

One of the most remarkable arrangements was from the hand of Erica Wyman. It consisted of the model of a caravan, and a large and rather muddy square of turf. Into this turf, stuck at random, were about a dozen rose-buds. While I was trying to puzzle out the significance of this curious piece, I noticed a card leaning against the caravan door. On it was written:

Where my caravan has rested
Flowers I leave thee on the grass.

So that was it. All most interesting, though perhaps somewhat unhygienic; she had omitted to remove a large worm which glared at me from the edge of the turf. However, it must certainly be mentioned. If it was not beautiful, it was at least ingenious.

It was time to do the lilies, for which a special place had been reserved on the centre table. They were soon finished; they were so beautiful that they arranged themselves. I was just dropping the last flower into place when a car drew up in the lane outside. A moment later the door was pushed open and in walked Miss Emily.

To say that she walked in is perhaps a misnomer, for she was staggering under a large object which looked like a sawn-off hip-bath. Which, indeed, was what it was. It was painted a vivid green, and fitted inside with an elaborate contraption of twisted wire-netting.

'Oh dear!' she panted. 'How very unfortunate! I had intended this to be a surprise!'

'I'm sorry,' I said. 'Would you like me to go?'

'No, indeed. I did not mean to be rude. In fact, I am very glad to find you here. Perhaps you would not mind helping me with the rest of the things from the car?'

The 'rest of the things' proved to be several large rocks, a bundle of wet moss which dripped on to my trousers, a watering can – and a suitcase. On being opened, this disclosed exactly what I had expected. Yes, there were the ixias, and the gladioli, and the tiger-lilies – all the flowers which she had been buying in Kenton.

'What beautiful flowers,' I remarked. 'And they don't seem to be at all damaged by the storm.'

'No,' replied Miss Emily, without batting an eyelid. 'They were all picked before it broke.'

Perhaps they were, I thought. But not by you.

She proceeded to make her arrangement. The hip-bath was so large that one end of it protruded over the trestle table, so that when she pushed the rocks to the edge it almost over-balanced. However, that was soon remedied. She then placed a number of pinholders among the rocks; they looked like green sea-anemones waiting for the tide to come in. After a bag of sand had been emptied over the bottom, she poured in a couple of cans of water. The bath was then ready for the reception of the flowers, which were stuck on to the pin-holders, mostly in an upright position, with small heaps of moss round the ends of their stalks.

'There!' she exclaimed, standing back and surveying her handiwork. 'How do you think it looks? Does it remind you of anything?'

It reminded me with startling clarity of a hip-bath filled with rocks and pin-holders. But one could not say that. I observed that it was most interesting, most unusual.

'But doesn't it suggest a title?'

I racked my brains while she waited for an answer. Nothing suggested itself. 'Thoughts in a Hip-bath' would scarcely please, nor would 'The Fatal Hip-bath'. What it should really be called, of course, was 'Murder in a Hip-bath', but that sounded too like Agatha Christie. It was a pity that one was not a surrealist, because then one could have called it 'Mother and Child' and left it at that.

'I should have thought it was obvious,' said Miss Emily, rather impatiently – 'Swan Lake!'

'Of course!'

'After the ballet, you know.'

I did.

'But does not "Swan Lake" call for some swans?'

'It does indeed,' she agreed. 'I have them here. Four beautiful little swans!'

Out of her handbag she produced four celluloid swans, which she placed on the water. They twirled round and round, in a crazy dance, before finally coming to rest against the rocks.

'This,' I thought, 'is a situation that could only be illustrated by Dali. Hip-baths, rocks, watering cans, damp trousers, artificial swans.'

'Of course,' purred Miss Emily, 'I don't suppose that dear Rose will approve of it. Not at all the sort of thing she goes in for. But I rather fancy it might catch the eyes of other people.'

It might indeed. If they leaned too closely over the sharp leaves which she had clustered round the gladioli, it would not only catch their eyes but put them out.

Hardly had she uttered these words than there was the sound of another car drawing up in the lane. A door slammed, and we heard a voice that was only too familiar. It was Our Rose. Now we were for it.

Rose entered the room backwards.

'Be careful, Frieda dear,' she cried, 'or you will crush it! No – there is plenty of room for it to get through the door if you will only hold it properly. There – that's better. Oh dear – one of the delphiniums has fallen. Never mind, there are plenty more. One last push – splendid! Now I think we will have it over here.'

The Czechoslovakian maid, looking even more browbeaten than usual, staggered to the nearest table and deposited her burden on it. Then Rose turned, and 'saw' us for the first time.

'My dears!' she exclaimed. 'How delightful to find you

here!' Her eyes rested for a moment on Miss Emily's hip-bath, whereupon she flinched violently and closed her eyes for a moment, in order that there might be no possible doubt as to what she thought of it. She was like one of those actresses of the silent films who, when registering disgust, screwed up their faces into contortions which suggested that their mouths were full of sour apples. Then, opening her eyes, she smiled bravely towards it. She did not look at it *directly* – for that, as she wished us to understand, would have been too much to expect of her. She looked slightly above it, as though it were a Gorgon's head. Then she murmured: 'So amusing!'

By these transparent manœuvres we were not impressed; they were part of the normal social intercourse of Meadow-stream, and could hardly be described even as impolite. Besides, we were too fascinated by Rose's own creation, which Frieda had just put down. This proved to be a large wicker bird-cage, some four feet high, from which there burst, at every angle, a dazzling display of rare flowers. There were delphiniums splendid enough for the most exclusive exhibitions, and long-stemmed roses, trimmed and wired, which had all the elegance of Bond Street. There was a carpet of gentians of a variety which Rose could not possibly have grown in her chalky soil, and a spray of golden fern only cultivated in a hot-house, which she did not possess.

There was a deadly silence. At last Miss Emily spoke.

'All out of the garden, dear?' she asked softly.

In equally dulcet tones Rose replied: 'I believe those are the rules.'

Then she stared, very deliberately, at the hip-bath. 'Your lovely gladioli! You must have been hiding them in your secret garden, dear, for I'm sure I've never seen them before.'

The two ladies glared at each other. Greek had met Greek. Both of them were tapping their feet, and both of them were pursing their lips, as though they were about to whistle.

Rose broke the tension. 'But Frieda,' she cried, 'where is Polly? Where is our sweet Polly? We left him in the car! Then we must get him *at once*, mustn't we? Or he might fly away!'

Frieda went out.

'So there is to be a bird in the cage?' demanded Miss Emily, who was bristling with curiosity.

'Of course there is to be a bird in the cage, dear. What would a cage be, without a bird?'

Miss Emily addressed her next remark to me. 'I had no idea this was to be an exhibition of livestock,' she observed, with an acid smile.

'If it comes to that,' retorted Rose, 'there are four birds in your bath. It *is* a bath, is it not?'

Miss Emily ignored this insult. 'I said livestock, dear.'

'Oh, I see!' Rose gave a tinkling laugh. 'You thought my sweet Polly was a real bird? Oh no, dear. Just a little thing that I stuck together.'

Frieda came in again, with the 'little thing'. It was a large macaw, most cunningly fashioned in everlasting flowers. It was a striking object, and a highly professional one, such as might have been expected of a student of Faberge, with its elaborate feathered tail, its painted feet, and its beady eyes. In Bond Street it would have cost – and probably did – at least ten guineas.

'It's remarkable what one can do with a little wire,' observed Rose, hanging Polly in the cage.

'Very remarkable.' Miss Emily regarded Polly with open hatred. 'Almost incredible.'

'Just a little patience, dear, that's all one needs.'

'Not quite *all*, dear, surely?'

'How do you mean?'

Miss Emily gave a mirthless laugh. 'I should have thought that other qualities were needed too.'

'Such as?'

'Never mind, dear.'

Rose shrugged her shoulders and turned her back. So did Miss Emily. That was how I left them, breathing heavily, ignoring one another, as though they were beings from a different planet.

I walked home through the lanes in a state of some disquiet. The prospect of judging the entries on the morrow was formidable indeed; whatever the decision it was bound to cause bitter heartburnings. If the prize went to Our Rose, Miss Emily would certainly never speak to me again; if it went to Miss Emily, Our Rose would never forgive me. I might declare a dead heat, and make a few graceful remarks about the impossibility of deciding between two such works of genius, but that would be a dreadful anti-climax; it would lack all those qualities of drama to which we had become accustomed. In the last resort, the prize might go to neither; it might be awarded to Miss Mint, or to the blood-stained woman with the honeysuckle, or to the young giant with the pansies. And one could explain to Rose and Emily, separately, that of course *she* should really have earned the prize, but that in the interests of democracy . . . oh dear, it was all very difficult. Perhaps things would appear easier in the morning, after a good night's sleep.

But even sleep seemed likely to be denied. For Mrs. Maples's cow – the exceptionally female one in the field opposite – had decided that this was a night, of all nights, when it must give an exhibition of mooing. That was bad enough during the day; at night it was intolerable, and all the more enraging because it had no real reason to moo at all. It had not had a calf taken away from it; it only *thought* it had. This peculiar illusion had been explained to me, with surprising frankness, by Our Rose on a previous occasion.

'It is what they call a *fausse couche*, my dear,' she said.

I suspected that Mrs. Maples's cowman might employ a different term, but I let it pass.

'So interesting, I always think. It happens in human beings, too, I believe. Something to do with the weather, I expect.'

Fausse couche indeed! What right had Mrs. Maples's cow to go fausse couching just under my window, when all these ghastly problems were coming to a head? That cows should have babies was in the nature of things; one would be the last to suggest that they should stop. To have imaginary babies was sheer affectation. To have them in French was worst of all. I should write to Mrs. Maples in the morning and suggest that her cow should see a psychiatrist.

With which consoling thought I went to bed.

§ I X

I was awakened by Gaskin at what felt like the crack of dawn, though it was, in fact, nearly eight o'clock.

'Mrs. Pattern is on the telephone,' he said.

'At this hour?'

'She won't go away. Says it's most urgent.'

I cursed and tumbled out of bed. As I went downstairs I noticed that it was going to be a glorious day, cool, clear and golden.

'Hullo?'

Her voice, over the telephone, sounded as if she were about to burst into tears.

'Oh Mr. Nichols . . . the most terrible thing . . . Mrs. Maples's cow . . .'

'What did you say?'

'Her cow . . . Mrs. Maples's . . .'

'What has happened to it?'

'The Assembly Rooms – the Flower Show – a complete wreck. . . .'

Then it all came out. At some time during the night Mrs.

Maples's cow, not content with mooing its head off in order to give expression to its tedious illusions, had escaped from its field, wandered up the lane, and penetrated to the garden of the Assembly Rooms. Somebody, it seemed, had left the doors open – thank heavens it could not have been me – and the cow, presumably thinking that it was entering a shed, had gone in and created unbelievable havoc.

'Every table overturned,' quavered poor Mrs. Pattern – 'vases smashed all over the floor – just like an earthquake. Hardly a single thing left standing – quite impossible to have the Show.'

'Oh dear . . . how terrible!' Even as I uttered these appropriate sentiments I was conscious of a lighter heart.

'We shall have to raise some sort of fund,' she went on, 'to compensate people. So many really valuable things gone. And I'm afraid that isn't all.'

'But what else has happened?'

'It must have broken into other places. They found an old hip-bath in the lane, and a sort of cage that must have been a hen-coop. What did you say?'

I said nothing. There are times when it is impossible to do so.

'Operator . . . operator. . . .'

I controlled myself. 'Yes, Mrs. Pattern?'

'Oh, there you are. We must have had a crossed line. I'm sure I heard somebody laughing.'

I nodded. But suddenly I felt – in an odd sort of way – absent-minded. For the sun was shining down the stairs, sparkling through the clear panes where once the stained-glass window had stood. It threaded its way through the curves of the old balustrade, and fell in a little golden pool near a bowl of roses. The simplest bowl imaginable; red roses, white roses, yellow roses, leaning together in fragrant affection.

'I thought I heard somebody laughing,' repeated Mrs. Pattern.

Yes. So did I. Somebody laughing. I could not take my eyes off the staircase . . . It was so pretty in the sunlight. That was where the laughter seemed to come from. I must go upstairs and dress, and go out into the garden. It was going to be a lovely day.

INDEX

The index of plant names was prepared by Roy C. Dicks. Plants are indexed by currently accepted botanical name. A cross-reference has been provided wherever the author used a common name or outdated Latin name.

·